Mid-Reach

Betsy Mack

A BOOK TO INSPIRE,
EMPOWER, AND
CELEBRATE FAILING
WHILE IN THE
MIDST OF SUCCESS

ISBN: 978-1-7333252-2-6 (hard cover)
ISBN: 978-1-7333252-5-7 (soft cover)
Edited by: Monika Dziamka and Amy Ashby

Cover photo by: Laurel Belle Photography

Published by Warren Publishing
Charlotte, NC
www.warrenpublishing.net
Printed in the United States

To my parents: For your endless
love and support; for always
believing in me, even when I wasn't
able to; for instilling in me kindness,
humility, morals, and respect;
and for encouraging my dreams,
that always grew like weeds,
to blossom into wildflowers.
Because of you, I am proud to be me.

And to all the girls with messy top knots,
long lashes, and high heels:
Keep your glasses filled with coffee
and your hearts filled with dreams.
You got this.

Mid-Reach

BETSY MACK

Table of Contents

Prologue

My name is Betsy Mack. No, you have never heard of me. I have not (yet) won any nationally accredited awards, never have I held the title of CEO, nor have I been featured in *Forbes* magazine. I am an average, young professional in the midst of my career with an undeniably strong drive, doing all that I am able in order to succeed in the business world.

I read business article after article, pour myself into best sellers, attend seminars, and circulate networking events. I have had the opportunity to meet many business and community leaders and learn from them firsthand. I have strong mentors who have helped to guide and impact my profession. I am fortunate to have a strong circle of influence, individuals who recommend other books to add to my library of business knowledge.

An overwhelming number of the books I read are written with a "top-level looking down" approach. This type of mentoring has been extremely influential thus far in my career. However, each book sparks the same questions in my mind. What should I be doing now? What are other people in the middle of their careers doing? What were those top business leaders doing when they were in the midst of their professions? And what if they had written a book before they became the Richard Bransons, Sheryl Sandburgs, Arianna Huffingtons, and Warren Buffets we now know, idolize, envy, and admire?

A book of reflection carries a different tone when compared to a book written about a situation in the heat and fury of it all. When writing from the top-down approach, you put on your rose-colored glasses and guide your readers through the path of your success, complete with challenges that become cliffhangers

Average

I am average.

My height, shoe size, grade point average, and test scores all point to average. It's simply a matter of fact. I am average. Have you cringed yet at that phrase? I have. It sounds so awful. But why? When did this word start to carry such a negative connotation?

By definition, average is the norm—an amount, standard, level, or rate regarded as usual or ordinary, the majority of the population. Simply stated, by this definition, most people are, in fact, average. Why then does being average feel like defeat? I've been average for the greater part of my life. All of my tests, charts, scores all pointed determinedly toward averageness. I never put too much focus into this notion until I entered high school. In high school, the labeling becomes more visible—a part of one's identity.

At my high school, students were immediately pushed into one of three categories: honors, those with special-needs, and everyone else. The honors students had the attention and expectations. Everyone presumed they would become leaders not only in the school, but also one day in the business world. Those students with special needs received the special attention and extra time they needed to excel. Then there were the rest of us. We were placed sporadically throughout the remainder of the classes, learning to pass but not to succeed.

I fell into this norm gracefully. I accepted my label of averageness, upheld passing grades, and continued on as a typical student. Despite falling in line and going through the motions in school, I sought out other outlets to enable myself to stand out and shine. I have never been one to sit back and let life carry me passively, to allow others to define me, to have situations create me. I learned a lot about myself and my competitive side from childhood gymnastics. And I continued to pursue sports as my way to stand out. But day in and day out, from the hallways and into the classrooms, I was average with no expectations. And that was a label I hated.

I had a teacher who did everything in her power to push me down further into this average existence. She would look at me quizzically whenever I did anything remotely well—including the time I finished a Sudoku puzzle first, on which she insisted I had cheated. If I were to do anything that exemplified me in a greater light, she would look at me with narrowed eyes. I still have yet to forget her exasperated response when I was laughing with friends about a mistake I had made on a test, to which she shouted out for the entire class to hear, "You're a ditz!" My look of shock prompted her to add, "If the shoe fits, wear it, girly."

Little did I know, that was the edge off of which I needed to be pushed. I began to try to prove to her that I was capable of more than what she thought. I knew I would never be at the top of my class. But I knew I was far from the girl she thought I was. I have always tried to think the best of my teachers in hopes that they were trying to motivate students to live up to their potential. However, it was clear in her undermining responses that in me, she saw no potential. I felt lost in the sea of others.

I advanced from high school with mediocre grades, went to a state university, and graduated with an average GPA. It was not until I started job searching that my true potential began to shine. I fixated my time on my future career. I knew that in school, despite taking different tracks or subjects, everyone was following the same standard curriculum. But jobs were different. Jobs were unique to skill sets, traits, expertise, strengths. And I wanted to find mine: my job I was uniquely good at, the job that would fit me best.

In one summer, I sent out ninety-eight different resumes to ninety-eight open jobs. I had nothing I could put on my resume that enabled me to break away and stand out. I tried to be creative with my cover letters or insert random facts that might have helped to push my resume to the top of the applicant pile. However, my submissions were left unanswered, which triggered in me the reaction of needing to send more.

I refused to fail. Every rejection letter motivated me to try harder. I was determined, focused, and knew I needed to find a job with possibility and opportunity. I needed a job to grow and learn. A job with a purpose. One that showed that while I was average in some areas, my averageness was not all-encompassing.

After months of relentless effort (and rejection, silence, and more rejection), I accepted a position with the United Way of Greater St. Louis. Was receiving the job a testament that I was no longer average? That I stood out where others did not? Hardly. What the job did do, however, was give me a new stage upon which to dance. A blank canvas where I could paint myself in a new light. An opportunity.

This new job was a role with leadership involvement, fundraising goals, public speaking opportunities, and the ability to learn. The job enabled me to grow personally and professionally. I advanced quickly through the organization, and my experience catapulted me into a new job at a new company at a director-level position in the corporate world. All of the exact highlights and accomplishments are outlined neatly on my resume. But what is not listed are the little things along the way that were instrumental in my success (which will be discussed in great depth in future chapters) and the numerous people who supported me, guided me, mentored me, and helped to mold me into the businesswoman I am today.

Despite the fact that I was and still am average in many regards, I learned I had the ability to shine in other facets. By being average, you have the opportunity to put in more work to stand out. By simply putting in a little more time, a little more effort, you are already standing out against your competitors, peers, and counterparts. The drive behind your abilities is the deciding factor that pushes you outside of your average box.

When I started working at United Way, I had to put in a lot of long hours. Working a thirteen-hour day multiple times in a week was not unheard of—more so, it was the norm. Working at a nonprofit, especially early in my career, enabled me to establish a solid foundation of experience and a strong work ethic.

Working with more than 3,500 C-level and senior leaders taught me more than you can imagine. It enabled me to learn about their backgrounds and helped me to understand their career paths, which led me to realize that while successful executives are at the top of their industries now, so many of these individuals started out where I did: as average students, eager to learn.

I began to idolize business leaders with whom I was able to work, teaching myself to mirror their best qualities. These were qualities that were not the norm, stood out, enabled their successes. I remember a CEO who invited entry-level employees to sit at the table. I remember a fellow board cabinet member who walked into every meeting early, prepared, and polished. Simultaneously, I found other leaders had highly unattractive qualities, which I observed in greater depth, reinforcing the detrimental effects these characteristics played.

I look back at the incident with my high school teacher and thank her for the heartless, verbal humiliation. It awoke a fire inside that enabled me to expand my perception of what it means to be average. The shoe actually doesn't fit, girly, because there are no limits or constraints on success. Being average is far from the negative connotation the word unfortunately holds.

Being average is powerful. It enables a person to blend in with their peers and counterparts. Better yet, it allows one to break away. The average mindset is unique in the fact that by doing anything outside of the "norm," one is no longer considered average. The term is just a label society places on people who are in the masses. It is not absolute; instead to be called "average" should be viewed as a challenge. This is my favorite part about labels—they are not constant, but fluid.

You're labeled as average? Great. All people are—some much less than others, in one area or another. One of my favorite quotes, from Albert Einstein, says it best: "Everybody is a genius. But if you judge a fish by its ability to climb a tree, it will live its whole life believing that it is stupid."

All people have areas in which they thrive as well as areas of average capabilities. So, find your strength. Find where you flourish. Find your standout moment so you shine in the light of "outstanding" and not "average." Find your strengths and leverage them, even if they surprise you or are not what you thought they would be. I learned and am continuing to learn so much about myself and my skill set as I continue my professional journey. I know now that I am thoughtful, I understand the importance of connecting with unique individuals, and I am good at networking, light conversation, and reading an audience. All people have their strengths, weaknesses, and areas of mediocrity.

Accept this truth and use it to catapult yourself into your next endeavors. Where do your talents lie? What unique qualities do you have that exude excellence? What areas of expertise do you have that others lack? And the most important question: how much effort and energy are you willing to put forth toward those talents? So often, our greatest leaders come out of an average background but possess an undeniably strong work ethic.

So, why not me? Better yet—why not you?

"I AM NOT MORE GIFTED THAN THE
AVERAGE HUMAN BEING. IF YOU KNOW
ANYTHING ABOUT HISTORY, YOU WOULD
KNOW THAT IS SO—WHAT HARD TIMES I
HAD IN STUDYING AND THE FACT THAT
I DO NOT HAVE A MEMORY LIKE SOME
OTHER PEOPLE DO ... I AM JUST MORE
CURIOUS THAN THE AVERAGE PERSON
AND I WILL NOT GIVE UP ON A PROBLEM
UNTIL I HAVE FOUND THE PROPER
SOLUTION. THIS IS ONE OF MY GREATEST
SATISFACTIONS IN LIFE—SOLVING
PROBLEMS—AND THE HARDER THEY ARE,
THE MORE SATISFACTION DO I GET OUT
OF THEM. MAYBE YOU COULD CONSIDER
ME A BIT MORE PATIENT IN CONTINUING
WITH MY PROBLEM THAN IS THE
AVERAGE HUMAN BEING. NOW, IF YOU
UNDERSTAND WHAT I HAVE JUST TOLD
YOU, YOU SEE THAT IT IS NOT A MATTER
OF BEING MORE GIFTED BUT A MATTER OF
BEING MORE CURIOUS AND MAYBE MORE
PATIENT UNTIL YOU SOLVE A PROBLEM."

—ALBERT EINSTEIN

Average is subjective, and I object to letting the label pull me down. I challenge you to acquire the same mindset. There are so many other qualities in a person that determine success. So, I gladly accept the "average" title. For all of you currently reading who are also average, do not succumb to the negativity surrounding the title. Instead, rise against it. Let's continue to bask in our average glory. I raise my glass to us. Continue being average and hold that label like a badge of pride. Because we will succeed. Maybe not all of us—but most definitely some of us. If nothing else, the odds are in our favor.

CHAPTER 2

Work Ethic

Ethics are moral principles. And your *work* ethic is *your* code of *your* principles, to be created by you, executed by you, and displayed by you. Work ethic is less about what you say and is entirely how you do it.

I am sure everyone knows the phrase, "Your work ethic is what you do when no one's looking." And thank goodness nobody is watching, because I don't need to feel personally attacked daily for the eight cups of coffee I may or may not drink while burrowed away working. But work ethic needs to be viewed as the input that gives you your output—the effort, time, and focus you put in to achieve the results you want, need, and have.

As mentioned, I was extremely fortunate to start my career at such a well-established and highly-respected organization, United Way. My work ethic came from the foundational lesson one of my team leaders at the time would repeat, that "if you're not fifteen minutes early, you're late." And while even now I am not always as timely as I would like to be, from the beginning of my career I was taught the importance of timely responses and proper business etiquette, such as how best to follow up with board minutes or the proper way to put together a meeting agenda. While work ethic is how you work, these little notions noted above were instrumental in displaying my work ethic.

I was sitting at Starbucks the other day, working on this little project, and I could not help but overhear two women talking. They were outraged by how their managers would question their work ethic. One of them stated, "HR called me into her office to talk because she heard me crying after my manager told me I was not adding value to the team. He is a bully, so I reported to HR how mean he was to me."

I am a firm believer that if someone is questioning your work ethic, you should question it as well. There is a reason why someone is inquiring. From your lack of presence to your shortage of output, there is a purpose behind the curiosity. And this is your opportunity to find that reason and reevaluate your strategy or behavior.

Taking a proactive approach is not always easy. Sometimes swallowing your pride and admitting you're not doing as well as you could be is hard. However, by taking the initiative to seek out cause for questioning and assume accountability, you will not only gain the respect of your superiors, you will have the opportunity to redefine your work ethic in a positive light.

Many people will advise you to be the first in the office and the last to leave. On one hand, that is fabulous advice. Take it, learn it, live it. On the other hand, there is so much that goes into this saying that many people forget. A strong work ethic is not going to be created by simply being seen. I have worked with a few people who were prime examples of this sentiment. They would be in the office before daybreak and would leave well after dark, often making jokes about changing their home address to the office. Yet, these were the individuals who would also take long lunches, often walk around in multiple departments making small talk, and would rarely sit at their idle computers.

But on the flip side, just as much as we are a society of results, we are still uncomfortable with lack of transparency and the unknown. Even with amazing results at work, an employee's physical absence can create a sense of ambiguity and, thus, doubt among the rest of the workforce. I have seen coworkers inquire about the efforts behind their successful yet non-present coworker.

Being seen is only half of the equation; output is the other. And yes, both sides are important. We all know those individuals who are always popping into others' cubicles or standing by the coffee maker. Because really, what do they do all day? It is all about balance.

The workweek is supposed to consist of forty hours. Does anyone actually experience such a schedule? I could probably count my forty-hour workweeks on one hand. Getting up early to brief myself on the news and staying up late to enter data and work on prospect lists are regular occurrences. It's not because my days are unproductive, quite the contrary. With days typically full of meetings that accommodate other people's schedules, I need to find off-hours to do the mundane, yet necessary tasks that have to be completed before the start of the following day. There are other early mornings or late nights when I find myself working not because I didn't have time during the typical 8 a.m. to 5 p.m. hours, but because I want to be further than where I currently am. When my results are low, I increase my activities.

But let's get right to the facts—I know, easier said than done. Like a landslide, a person can find him or herself falling into a lazy routine, getting caught up in social hour, or leaving work five (okay, fine, thirty) minutes early. Building a strong work ethic is a process and one that can be seen as a journey without a true destination.

My work ethic continues to push me into developing qualities that display my efforts. One of the most vital and valuable skills I mastered was learning how to prospect for new donors. I learned how to create a personal connection and leverage that bond to establish a relationship. This single aspect alone has notably driven success in my current career.

> "YOUR WORK ETHIC IS DEFINED
> THROUGH A REPETITION OF ACTIONS.
> MAKE SURE THOSE ACTIONS ARE
> SOMETHING YOU WANT TO BE KNOWN FOR."

One of my little secrets (and weekly goals) is to reach out to five people who were highlighted in the current week's *Business Journal*. I pick five stories—sometimes headliners and other times short side features—and I send a personal letter to these five individuals, picking out something that inspired me about their article that hopefully establishes a personal connection and helps to personify me. Are they too, from the Quad Cities? Are they a Yankees fan who just so happens to be playing my team (Go, Cubs, go!) that night? Do they also enjoy reading? (Which by the way, have you read <insert book of the week here>?)

The importance of personifying yourself with strangers is imperative. This aspect enables you to create yourself as more than just a name on a piece of paper and as more than just a phone number belonging to yet another cold caller. And it is another way to exemplify your work ethic. It shows you genuinely care about the people with whom you hope to do business and you are willing to take a step beyond what others may be doing to connect with them.

I have sent a lot of hand-written, personal letters, averaging 250 a year. Not all letters have led to a new donor/prospect/client; however, these letters have sparked some great conversations, introduced some fabulous referrals, and, most importantly, instilled in me a strong work ethic.

One of the most important things about work ethic is it shows consistency in what you do, how you work, and the effort you put forth. Your work ethic should be what you do in front of your boss as well as in a closed-door office. Your work ethic is defined through a repetition of actions. Make sure those actions are something you want to be known for.

When I managed a board of directors, I had to keep more than fifty people informed, engaged, and updated. With fifty different, jam-packed schedules, it was understood that not every member attended every meeting. Therefore, I would send out full agendas prior to the meeting, complete with handouts for people to review beforehand. Board members received their standard welcome of a name tag and a packet of all documents to be discussed (color-coded, obviously). After the meetings, I would send out a full recap within two hours, complete with action items and next steps.

None of the actions described above were groundbreaking or revolutionary, however, they provided consistency, especially for any volunteers. I've attended board meetings that executed consistent practices and I have also attended meetings that did not. Both were conducted successfully. However, by putting in the extra effort and the additional hours to provide a more consistent, engaging, and organized structure, I was able to lead my meetings in a manner that demonstrated my dedication to the cause and to everyone present, including my volunteers.

Sometimes, enabling people to see your work ethic is not so easy. Sometimes, it is the late nights of entering data or the early-morning emails that need your focus. The people who you want to notice all your hard work aren't always going to see your efforts. But your work ethic should never be centered on the need to be seen, praised, or admired. Trust that your efforts will pay off. Because even if they are not recognized by individuals, your efforts will be validated through a track record of success.

While still at United Way, I moved successfully through the company and its divisions. I began my career in a small, remote office that enabled me to be the big fish in the small pond. Although we were all in the same role, I had power where my peer counterparts in the large, corporate office did not. I had the C-level's ear, while my colleagues were lucky if they were able to speak to mid-level managers. Despite the perception of my job having more influence, it was quite the opposite. Their clients were larger, and their pace was faster.

Still, working in this smaller office gave me an undeniably vital start. It allowed me to develop and grow quickly. I was able to control my environment, assess needs, and respond accordingly. I was able to push things forward a lot more quickly and learn how to evaluate my work. I was able to impact my (notably smaller) bottom line at a much greater rate than those in the corporate office. And because of this factor, I was able to learn quickly. However, I also grew to he point where my success could be repeated easily and I became complacent. I needed to continue to be challenged, and that would need to come from change.

I sought out my current boss as well as my future boss to initiate a switch to a lateral position. Moving over to the corporate office enabled me to shine in a different light. I was able to develop a different set of skills that the position demanded. I was also placed in front of a new audience. I was making a name for myself in the corporate office, with my colleagues, and with our board members and volunteers.

This move was a true breakthrough for my career. The one driving factor that sparked the interest in this change was my work ethic. That is where the will to lead became apparent. Never let yourself settle. Never let yourself become complacent in your career. I learned early on that I need challenges to encourage growth. In this instance, my situation was ideal—a new position to evoke new challenges. However, I also learned new challenges do not always present themselves. More often than not, I find myself in my current work role needing challenges, needing goals, needing new projects. And sometimes, these opportunities for growth simply do not exist.

So, go find one. Create your own opportunity.

You want to bring on new clients? Set a goal, then rely on your work ethic to crush it. You want to bring on five new clients? Reach out to 200 people through four different platforms (email, real mail, social media, networking events) with seven different touch points. Do these suggestions seem like a lot of work? They are. But your work ethic and dedication will be visibly apparent. In this case, there is no science behind these numbers. I am just throwing them out there to show the importance of what it takes, and it is always double if not quadruple the work you think it will be. However, as mentioned in the previous chapter, putting in this extra effort will help you to break away from being average and place yourself in a new light. So, put in exponentially more work than what you are expected to do. And after you do that, do more.

With that said, there needs to be a balance. Push hard, then allow time to recoup. Most of the business books I have read will tell you the opposite. They will tell you to continue to push, always expand, and never contract. They will tell you that if you for one second let yourself relax, your competition will pounce and claim victory. I strongly disagree with this kind of sentiment. If in your career you are always pushing, always expanding, always focusing on the next task, project, goal, challenge, you will burn out. Allow your career to have ebbs and flows.

And this is exactly what I learned to do. I learned how to push myself to work 110 percent while challenging my abilities and myself. Then I learned how to coast.

It is not as easy as it sounds to want results and then force yourself to slow down. However, I am a firm believer in the importance of this approach to balance. As a runner, I relate my career work ethic to my workouts.

When I ran cross-country in school, my coach developed intense interval track trainings for our team. These workouts would consist of a hard 600-meter sprint, followed instantly by a 200-meter slow jog. That was half of a mile and counted as one rep. Four reps would equal one set. And one practice would consist of three to seven sets. Sometimes our sprint would be 400 meters followed by a 400-meter jog, and other times our workouts would be 700 meters on the sprint and a 100-meter recovery jog. The sprints, while seemingly more important, were equally as essential to the workout as the recovery lap. Regardless, these workouts gave us the endurance to run for a longer distance. These sets would build the stamina we needed for our ten-mile or longer runs.

Your career is a marathon built of sprints and jogs; all-out surges, and recovery laps. Both are needed to create a balanced work ethic that will create a well-rounded career journey. Sometimes your sprints will need to be long and daring with a short recovery jog, and other times this may not be the case. The trick is to learn when you should push and then know the time you can allow yourself to decelerate. Having a strong career with comfortable and intelligent ebbs and flows takes patience and practice. But if you stay committed and dedicated, you will succeed. Because this is not just your career path; it is your journey.

CHAPTER 3

Mentors

The term *mentor* comes from Greek mythology. Described in Homer's epic *The Odyssey*, Mentor was in charge of teaching and supervising Telemachus, who was the son of Odysseus, the king of Ithaca, while Odysseus was away at war. When Telemachus became a young man, Goddess Athena visited him, disguised as Mentor. Athena gave Telemachus encouragement and practical plans for dealing with personal dilemmas, also leading him to learn more about his father.

Throughout generations, *mentor* has been adopted into English as a term for someone who imparts wisdom to and shares knowledge with a less-experienced, often younger person or colleague.

I believe now more than ever, mentors are prevalent in the business world. As I look back on my career thus far, I can think of many people to thank for having had a large helping hand in my success. Mentorship has become a hot topic; almost all well-known speakers talk about and thank their own mentors who have helped to guide and influence them. The cases are few and far between when any given speaker or key figure in business does not mention at least one specific mentor who has helped them in their success.

It seems leaders always have a mentor. But no one quite gives you the playbook on how to acquire one. If there is a sign-up sheet being passed around, I must have been out sick the day it came my way. Sometimes it feels as though everyone has been blessed with a full-on guidance counselor/therapist, while I am walking around like, "Hi, will you be my Yoda?" All of the business leaders I admire already have a full-time, eighty-hour workweek. Who has time to add another project to a never-ending, ever-growing to-do list?

When I started at United Way, I was twenty-two and green. I was extremely lucky to have Missy as my first boss and, consequently, my first unofficial mentor. Missy was about ten years older than I was, with an unmistakably strong track record of success. Missy also had some of the greatest attributes of any boss I have ever had. She challenged me to succeed, but did not let me settle. She gave me the spotlight when I deserved it, celebrated with me when I succeeded, and redirected me when I made mistakes.

While working with Missy, I had the responsibility of raising $1.1 million, organizing four large community events, and managing a board of local C-level leaders. At twenty-two, sitting in a room with twenty executives was more than slightly intimidating. To a somewhat doubtful board, Missy instilled confidence in my skill set.

A few board meetings in particular stand out to me as defining moments in my career. Walking into the boardroom at my first solo meeting and my second-ever board meeting, I felt unnerved. (Why do we have to motion to approve everything? Did that man just "nay"?) Missy reiterated the (now glaringly obvious) importance of being overly prepared. I went through my meeting notes multiple times and studied everyone's name, company, title, and picture. However, despite being overly prepared, I remained on edge. Most of these individuals were long-time board members who possessed a colossal wealth of knowledge with which I could not compete.

The meeting started well. I was able to greet every person by name and knew enough about each company to make the awkward small-talk conversations that always happen pre-assembly. The meeting began, and I had everyone's full attention. As we progressed, I began to receive questions from the members. They asked about the organization, the office, last year's funds, and more. I was able to answer the questions with confidence and continue the meeting.

Afterward, as a few individuals left, they congratulated me on my new role and emphasized their appreciation of my knowledge about the organization. That is when it hit me: the board members hadn't asked me any questions they didn't already know the answers to—they had asked me questions to make sure I had answers and was prepared.

Missy confirmed my suspicion. The board members, strong supporters and advocates for the organization, wanted to ensure their newest liaison would reciprocate their knowledge and passion. Missy had known the board would have high expectations of me. Though it had ultimately been my responsibility to lead the meeting successfully, she had armed me with the resources and tools to thrive.

Think of baseball. A coach would never send a player up to bat with a feather. However, just because a coach sends in his player with a brand-new wooden bat, does not guarantee the player is going to hit a home run. It's the combination of several aspects that leads to victory. In baseball, the bat, the player, the coach, the preparation, and the practice all contribute to a winning game. It is the coach's responsibility to assess the conditions, the other team, and know when to send in a player, but it is a player's role to be prepared. In business, it is the same. And Missy set me up to succeed, a key characteristic of a strong mentor.

As I was promoted to a different position at United Way and worked under the management of other individuals, I still stayed closely connected to Missy. She not only taught me a lot about business, but also proved to be a great all-around resource, friend, ally, listener, and supporter. Despite the informality of our relationship, Missy was my first real mentor in business. And for that, I am still extremely grateful.

As I reflect back on this time, many imperative questions arise in my mind. Does a mentor relationship need to be a formal situation? Should you ask an individual to be your mentor? How do you ask someone to be your mentor? And most importantly, who do you ask? Because what actually constitutes a mentor?

I started spiraling down a rabbit hole and it all only lead to more uncertainties.

My colleagues and I have had very insightful conversations around this subject. We agree a mentor is anyone who guides and influences you. While some people have formal mentors, informal mentorship works just as well. The most important part of mentorship is having a person who:

1. YOU CAN TRUST AND RELY ON;
2. CHALLENGES YOU FOR THE BETTER;
3. IS IN A ROLE YOU STRIVE TO BE IN, A PROFESSIONAL POSITION YOU IDOLIZE, OR OTHERWISE HAS ATTRIBUTES FROM WHICH YOU WANT TO EMULATE OR LEARN.

We all have those relationships in which we have someone to turn to, but we already know the advice we are going to receive. I have a fabulous group of friends and colleagues. But I also know them well enough to know to whom I can go when I want a certain type of response. Do I want someone to agree with me in a sympathetic manner? Do I want tough love? What about someone who will give me a dramatic dialogue comparable to a script from *Gossip Girl*? And sometimes I just want someone who will tell me I am right (even if I know I am really, really not).

Here is a realization I have come to accept, a game changer for me: the best mentors are not your biggest cheerleaders.

☙

So, I initiated a lateral job change that moved me from a satellite office to the corporate headquarters. However, after a year in this role, establishing myself in the position, meeting incredible leaders, and outlining my career path—which included the next step I would undoubtedly take—I was approached about a different opportunity.

Orvin, who was at that time leading the department of major gifts and responsible for a third of the organization's entire seventy-plus-million-dollar annual campaign, asked me to join his team. My first reaction was frustration (odd reaction, I know). But in my mind, my career path had already been set, which ever so conveniently included my next move. This change, while a promotion, was a huge side step in a direction I had not considered going. I sought out feedback from a few trusted friends and colleagues and was advised to take the position. And what a great decision that was.

Orvin was an intimidatingly strong leader. In our first meeting, we discussed goals and opportunities. He told me two things I will never forget: the first was to lean in to my job, and the second was more personal. Orvin told me to relax. "Be your authentic self," he said.

One time, during a meeting, he asked me what I was reading. I stared back at him, wondering if I should lie and tell him I was reading the newest business best seller or if I should be honest about the fact that Jennifer Weiner currently occupied my nightstand with another one of her "can't stop reading" soap opera-style novels. I opted for neither of the two choices and replied with the lame answer of "nothing …" to which Orvin responded, to my surprise, with: "Find something. Read an article that teaches you something and type up a short paragraph on what you learned." I thought, *What? This is not high school, and I do not need a homework assignment.* I went home that day feeling a little disgruntled, but nevertheless, I began working on my new task.

While trying to find an article that impressed me, let alone an article that would impress my soon-to-be-CEO boss, I realized I enjoyed reading. I read article after article. I found podcasts that were insightful and books that were inspirational. I do not remember the exact article I chose to read, nor do I remember what facts I typed up for my summary to Orvin. But somewhere along the way, I discovered his real mission: to inspire me to read and continue to learn, and to find my passion through continuing education. And thus began my new desire to fill my shelves with books and my head with knowledge. This is consequently when I realized Orvin would be an unexpected mentor in my life.

Through this new role with United Way, I gained additional skills that helped me to succeed. Despite my initial reaction of feeling uncertain with my career change, it was ultimately the best possible move for my career. I learned a career path is, as Sheryl Sandberg describes it, a jungle gym. And sometimes it takes a respected friend, colleague, or mentor to help you see the different routes of possibility you can take.

While on Orvin's team, I had one volunteer chair member with whom I worked closely. Her name was Marilyn, a top executive at a large corporation, a known community leader, the recipient of numerous awards, and highly-successful in every single aspect of the word. We collaborated to raise more than $6.5 million and host five large events. Marilyn and I clicked immediately. Marilyn respected and empowered me while completely inspiring me along the way. Together we worked long hours—workweeks that involved far more than forty hours—exchanging emails at all times of the day (okay, fine, night), and held sporadic meetings to review our spreadsheets. As the United Way staff liaison, I felt obligated to answer Marilyn's needs and requests—because after all, this was my job, and she was just a volunteer. Through this experience, our relationship was built on trust, reliability, and dependence.

The year's hard work paid off. Not only did we meet our goal, we exceeded it. And Marilyn and I formed a true relationship that was both a friendship and a mentorship. Marilyn again proved to be a huge asset to me as I later dealt with career challenges and needed business advice. Having a mentor like Marilyn was extremely important to my development; I was able to see myself in her, with my own hopes that my outcome as a leader in both the office and the community would replicate hers.

I was not always so lucky with my mentors, though. During one of my career moves, I started working with a CEO who had been on my list (yes, I have a list) of CEOs I aspire to know, work with, learn from. I could not have been more thrilled when she asked me to work with her, hoping that, as with many of my previous bosses, she too would become a mentor.

Working closely with this woman, I eagerly awaited the pivotal moment when I would learn from this mentor as I did with both Missy and Orvin. But she would either give me advice or provide me with insights I already knew or was not quite sure I agreed with. I was internally frustrated, blaming myself for not asking her the right questions.

Slowly, our relationship evolved, but not necessarily in a positive direction. The advice turned into interrogation. Whereas my previous accomplishments would receive approval followed by advice, they were now followed with doubt. She questioned the integrity of my sales in that perhaps my success came from my appearance, rather than my knowledge. "Because us pretty girls have to accept that," she told me.

> "YOUR MENTOR RELATIONSHIPS SHOULD MIMIC A BOARD OF DIRECTORS. FIND SEVERAL INDIVIDUALS WHO HELP TO GUIDE AND ADVISE YOU. NEVER CONFUSE SUCCESS AS A STATE IN WHICH YOU HAVE ALL THE ANSWERS."

I began to doubt my own success. This new mentor had become my voice of reason and moral compass; I held her word above all else. After winning two awards, I was thrilled to share the news with her. I called my mentor, and she responded in a way that felt like a slap in the face. "Well, there is another feather in your hat," she said. "I'm glad you're making a name for yourself, but what about the company?" To me, my success and the company's success were one in the same.

Through this experience, I learned so many things. First, I learned sometimes people are not who you think they are. And that's okay. And secondly, I realized just how important it is to diversify your mentors. I always knew having mentors from different backgrounds, different mindsets, and different industries was important to help provide unique perspectives. However, I did not realize how detrimental it would be to work with only one mentor, giving them the end-all, be-all say in the matter at hand.

People tell you to get a mentor. Singular. Once you have one, they don't tell you to continue to find more. My situation taught me how mentor relationships should mimic a board of directors. Find several individuals who help to guide and advise you. Never confuse success as a state in which you have all the answers. Having this woman as my mentor and seeing her personal success, I thought her advice, while not always new or needed, was generally the correct course of action for me to take.

After our relationship ended, I spent weeks in self-reflection. I did not accept my own accountability in this situation. I had not properly vetted the situation or this leader before jumping in with both feet, instilling full trust, and ultimately giving over the reins of my career. Before taking on a new role or position, or investing in a person, make sure the experience is one you need/want. And it is okay if you realize it's not (even if, like me, that realization comes after you jump forward).

The ending of this era brought me back to several old relationships, and it led me to many more that were new. I refreshed my insights on the significance of having a mentor with an identical work ethic to my own; an admirable drive and an enviable reputation are crucial. Marilyn, on the other hand, continues to provide advice that is influential, and it usually comes with validations that still resonate strongly with my professional choices. Marilyn continues to be a constant in my career. Despite no longer working in close proximity, simply knowing Marilyn reminds me what hard work can amount to.

I have always been lucky to have a contact list of some truly successful leaders. At a local business event, I ran into one of my former chairmen and the current company president, Seth. We quickly caught up, exchanged pleasantries and new business cards, and continued on our way. A few days later, I received a congratulatory email requesting a meeting and the offer to mentor me (not all in one fell swoop, but close enough).

Seth and I had a fabulous mentor relationship. It was a mentorship that the definition of the word itself would envy. It was, without a doubt, the most structured mentorship relationship I have ever had. We met like clockwork—once a month. We met at the same place—Starbucks. We held structured conversations— exchanging *New York Times* articles, discussing best-selling books, and alternating business topic conversations (Millennials, social media, women as leaders).

Seth was an extremely passionate and influential leader. I received great advice from him in various areas. He always provided insight for my career based off of his career experience. He always left me with much to think about and reflect on.

Seth once told me he loved collecting and recording random facts. These facts could be about anything—what type of a work-life balance people have; how many Baby Boomers would retire that year; the amount of touch points needed to create an impact. Regardless of their subject, the facts always consisted of a number and an interesting jumping point into a larger discussion. Slowly, I started collecting and sharing random facts as well, citing my sources and keeping these one-liners in a small journal that was always steadily filling up. Eventually, I started pulling out these facts in meetings and at networking events. They usually prompted (and still do) insightful discussions with interested individuals. Another fact I would soon like to add to my ever-growing list is how many people follow up on making lists of their own (which is hopefully an ever-growing list in itself).

Through my mentorships, I have gained a wealth of knowledge. Selfishly, I benefit immensely from these relationships. But while these individuals invest in me, I am hopeful that they too are able to benefit from our conversations.

In my meetings with Seth, we talked openly. As a Baby Boomer, he often directly asked for my opinion as a Millennial on a number of issues. As we communicated,

I spoke my mind and gave honest answers, even if I did not necessarily see the intellectual value Seth would gain from my responses. Several weeks after one such conversation, which was about social media, Seth followed up with me to let me know a comment I had made initiated a chain of events that led to a strategic change within the company.

This example with Seth is a true testament to the importance of mentorship in terms of reverse mentoring. While I see myself as the true winner in the relationship, wholly benefitting from his guidance, it is neat to see the inverse impact I can have on him and the company at large. Because of this experience, I feel obligated to provide my mentors with value. To other people, sometimes that value may be more impactful than at other times, but that is the beauty of intellectual worth—it is defined by its importance to the user. So, invest in your conversations with your mentors, and let the other person collect what they may want or need from your insight and honesty.

◦◦◦

Let's get to the point. How does someone find a mentor? My most recently acquired mentors are Tina and Lisa, my friends, confidantes, and two women I look up to in the business world. With both Lisa and Tina, it was simple: we opened up to each other, gained trust, were vulnerable, provided insight, and empowered each other. Real talk: we talked about bad days and specific challenges, drank wine, laughed, and shared personal stories about our families, relationships, and life goals. I met both of these women through a nonprofit board seat. And while I did not ask them to become my mentors, the bond advanced in such a way that neither woman needed the official title of "mentor." But just in case, I may just shoot them both a text right now to let them know of their roles in my life.

If you admire someone, ask that person to be your mentor. Not right away! Asking someone you've never met to be your mentor is slightly like asking someone on a first date to marry you. (Which, hey—if it works, it works! But for me, it doesn't work ....) Find that person, ask them to coffee a few times, and be prepared with an agenda and a list of questions. Everyone loves to talk about themselves (which is something I learned through exchanging hand-written letters). So, let them talk! Soak up the knowledge while you sip your coffee, take notes, and learn from their experience.

Here is how I've learned to secure a meeting:

1. WRITE A HANDWRITTEN LETTER. (SURPRISE! THE POST OFFICE IS STILL AROUND, AND WE NEED TO KEEP IT THAT WAY.)
2. INCLUDE SOMETHING IN THE LETTER YOU ADMIRE ABOUT THIS PERSON, WHY YOU WANT TO MEET. (DID HE OR SHE RECENTLY WIN AN AWARD? GAIN NEW BOARD-ROLE ACCOMPLISHMENTS? HELP MAKE NOTABLE COMPANY EARNINGS? SPEAK AT A WOMEN'S CONFERENCE AND ENCOURAGE OTHERS TO SIT AT THE TABLE? PUT THAT FACT IN THERE!)
3. COMPLIMENT THEM! (SAYING YOU ADMIRE THEM, VALUE THEIR INSIGHTS, STRIVE TO LEARN FROM THEM—IT IS HONEST BUT ALSO IMPORTANT TO REITERATE.)
4. ASK FOR WHAT YOU WANT. (BE DIRECT. I LOVE REQUESTING A TWENTY-MINUTE COFFEE MEETING BECAUSE TWENTY MINUTES IS NOT A HUGE BREAK TO A DAY. AND ALSO, COFFEE. PRETTY MUCH EVERYONE CAN USE A COFFEE BREAK! BECAUSE WHEN I HEAR COFFEE, I AM LIKE YEP, SIGN ME UP ASAP, THANKS.)

Recently, many people have reached out to me to ask for career advice. And I respond to every single request. It takes courage to reach out! I try to dedicate thirty minutes each week to any one individual who is pursuing a new job, has a question regarding the industry, is just starting his or her career search, or just needs someone to talk to or provide guidance.

If you are in a middle-management position or higher, reach out to that determined intern in your office or that college graduate down the street. Ask them what they are currently learning, inquire about challenges they are facing, ask about their career goals. Open the door for conversation and provide the opportunity for them to ask you questions they may otherwise be too scared to ask.

I am so lucky to be where I am today, thanks to other people who pushed me forward and believed in me. Most women don't have that kind of support. Women experience so much adversity, especially toward upward mobility. The work environment is hard enough; we need to support each other, build each other up, mentor each other.

After wrapping up a project, a colleague jokingly repeated a (butchered form of a) famous saying to me: "A high tide raises all ships." I laughed and went about my day. Months later, it popped back into my head. Realization hit me like a fast ball to the face. If we lift each other up, we all benefit. By mentoring others, through encouraging, empowering, and advising, we raise the standard. I addressed the issue of being average earlier—because I think I am, and maybe you are too. Think about it—if we collectively (for lack of a better word) all work together, we raise the bar. We raise the average. Sometimes, we rise simply by lifting others. The best part is, when that happens, we all benefit.

Mentorship has neither a job description, nor that little sign-up sheet (though I'm still not opposed to creating one). It isn't a one-size-fits-all product like that tacky sweater from the '80s. Let your mentor relationships grow at their own pace, whether they are organically created through management or sought out through external organizations. Just make sure your mentors provide these three things: 1. Trust, 2. challenges to make you better, and 3. they are in a role you strive to be in, are in a position you idolize, or have attributes from which you want to learn. And for fun, let's just add a fourth—coffee!

CHAPTER 4

Opportunities

In the business world, very few things are better than hearing the magical word, "opportunity." Opportunity—what an inspirational and motivational word, filled with so much promise and possibility! As defined, an opportunity is an advantageous chance, having favorable conditions; it is a set of circumstances that makes it possible to do something.

When I was initially offered the job at United Way, it was, as simply stated, an *opportunity*. When I was approached by a CEO outside of United Way and asked to join a small IT company at a director-level position on their executive team, it was (say it with me) an *opportunity*. When that same company allowed me to move halfway across the country to open a new office, in a new metro, it was (drum roll, please) an *opportunity*.

Let's reflect back on the definition of the word, opportunity: an advantageous chance, favorable conditions, circumstances that make something possible. This terminology creates a terrible misconception of the word. The description generates the fallacy that opportunities are given to us, that opportunities happen, and that opportunities are passive. Were the opportunities I described above given to me? Absolutely. Were they given by chance? Absolutely not.

After being employed at a St. Louis-based IT company for a year, I realized that while I was doing great work, I had outgrown the market. The company was growing and hoping to continue to expand into new markets. The CEO had made multiple comments about how she would love it if she could clone me and send me out into six other new metros to open offices there. So, I took her up on her word—

thankfully not on the cloning (I don't think the world would want, or be able to handle, any more of me), but on the opportunity to open a new office.

I approached her regarding the possibility of leading the company through our national expansion, moving to a new city, and opening up an office. She was thrilled. She encouraged me to go visit different cities, start doing research, and begin to decide on which area I would like to focus. If I had not prompted the discussion, would I have ever been approached about this opportunity? Maybe. But it would not have happened as quickly if I had not pursued it. This was a true opportunity. I was determined to invest the energy, effort, and time toward ensuring this opportunity would come through to fruition. And it did. But it did not happen solely out of chance.

> "YOU DON'T LIKE THE DIRECTION IN WHICH YOU ARE HEADED? SWITCH LANES. BETTER YET—SWITCH ROADS, SWITCH ROUTES, SWITCH CARS. I THINK THIS IS THE MOST INSPIRATIONAL ASPECT OF FATE AND DESTINY IN RELATION TO OPPORTUNITIES: YOU CAN CREATE THEM. "

While opportunities may be created, presented, or simply just happen, there are many factors that go into them. No one said it better than the Roman philosopher Seneca: "Luck is what happens when preparation meets opportunity." When broken down, this wise sentiment reinforces the idea that if you work hard to prepare—with a whole lot of determination, work ethic, and perseverance—and opportunity presents itself, that is luck.

I hate to bring luck into the equation, but it is (perhaps unfortunately) a true variable. Will opportunities present themselves without luck? Maybe. Are people who receive opportunities simply just lucky? Maybe. Still, luck is the chance that helps to create the opportunity. In any case, I hope we can all agree that preparation is a key element. If any opportunity becomes available, if one is not prepared, one will not succeed.

Now, I do believe in destiny and fate. But I also believe it is you who controls your own destiny. You don't like the direction in which you are headed? Switch lanes. Better yet—switch roads, switch routes, switch cars. I think this is the most inspirational aspect of fate and destiny in relation to opportunities: you can create them. And by switching out any element of the equation, you can produce a whole new outcome.

It is easy to sit back and watch others "fall into" new opportunities. And to be fair, some people truly do just that. They are in the right place, at the right time, with the right knowledge and the right responses. And how fabulous to be one of those people. (And yet, how mundane and boring.) But I would argue the vast majority of successful people do not simply stumble upon their opportunities. As stated before, they create them.

Creating opportunities is about building your brand, reinforcing your work ethic, and enabling others to see your achievements and potential. As discussed in the previous chapter, work ethic is what you consistently do and the person you consistently are. Work ethic is a reputation composed through repetition.

The first step to creating opportunity is identifying what you want. Opportunities are not like blindly throwing darts at a bullseye. Motivations drive the occasions, and potential lives within the chances. Discover your ideal aspiration. Is there an open position you want to be considered for? Do you need additional growth in your current role? Are you hoping to be recognized by your executive team? Would you like to be seen in the community as a mover, a shaker, a leader? By identifying your goal, you can begin to create the strategy around how to get there. Be deliberate and calculated about your approach.

I have learned a lot about the strategy of positioning myself for opportunities. Do everything with a purpose while still being genuine in your actions. At United Way, I had the ability (but more so the opportunity) to meet with various business leaders to cultivate donors, meet prospects, and otherwise formulate relationships. Was meeting with these individuals a part of my required job? No. Was I forced to set up these meetings to adequately complete my job? No. Could I have successfully achieved my goals and objectives without setting up these individual meetings? Absolutely. So, why set up these meetings? Why put in more work and effort to do something that would only indirectly help achieve my work goals? Because by setting up these meetings, I was able to meet these untouchable, admired business leaders and have their undivided attention for a full thirty minutes or more. I was able to learn more about them and how they made their own professional starts. I was able to selfishly put my name on their radar while unselfishly promoting and advocating for United Way.

While I was still working for the United Way, I was reading my weekly edition of the *St. Louis Business Journal*, when I noticed a small side article about a woman who had started a new company in St. Louis. The article detailed her accomplishments and neatly outlined her passion for the community. Amazing. She was a perfect prospect for the United Way's Women's Leadership Society, and here was an incredible opportunity for me to learn about this woman's journey to success.

I reached out to her through a hand-written letter, requesting a twenty-minute meeting and including my business card. She responded a week later, and we met for coffee. I was successful in learning more about her, introducing myself, and securing a brand-new, major monetary gift for the Women's Leadership Society.

I was able to successfully align my job's goal of raising money by connecting with our current donors to ask for increased gifts, and meeting prospects to ask for first-time donations, with my personal goal of face time with individual business leaders. I was strategic in my meetings, coming in with fully-prepared agendas. I would ask these leaders about themselves, their backgrounds, their motives, their successes, their challenges, their passions. I was eager to learn, and they were willing to share.

I realized at the time that I was fortunate to be able to position myself to hear from some of the most successful industry leaders. I was strategic in creating situations that would benefit the company as well as myself. Through these meetings, my division gained exponential growth, and I met with my personal most-admired leaders. The lesson: take advantage of situations your job generates.

In a previous role, I had been required to attend five large networking events that consisted strictly of C-level and senior-level executives. The events were created to feel intimate, enabling attendees to truly connect with the leaders in the room. I was expected to not only meet them, but successfully sell to them as well. Now, prior to any large networking event, I identify five people with whom I will talk. Notice I said *will* talk to—not *hope to* talk to. Place yourself in the mindset of *doing* and not *wanting*.

I am not naïve enough to believe I am the only person attending these events with a strategy in hopes of walking away with business, introductions, strong conversations, and a sale. Anyone who has no such expectation should reevaluate his or her purpose for attending.

Think about football. No player would ever go into the game without assessing the field, their opponents, the game plan, and their route. Each and every variable creates an impact that could deter or promote your outcome. Walking into a conference, may it be one that lasts two hours or two days, with little or no knowledge of the situation, attendees, or environment, will leave you to rely on sheer luck alone. And as we discussed before, only very few people get by on luck alone. Don't be one who counts on it.

Even today, as I attend my various work events, knowing I will, once again, be one of many, many people present, I have to be extremely tactical and systematic in my approach to meet my target individuals. As I said, do everything with a purpose behind it. After identifying my five individuals, I research them intently. Where did they go to college? Does that college have a big rivalry game coming up? Does that college play in the same division as my favorite team? The internet is a beautiful, creepy little thing. So many facts are at your fingertips, literally. Use those facts to your advantage!

Notice this is the same approach I revealed earlier—it is personifying yourself in a manner that enables you to break away, stand out, and be noticed. Let me know which statement is more memorable:

1. "NICE TO MEET YOU, FRANK. PLEASE TELL ME ABOUT YOUR COMPANY."
2. "THERE IS A BIG UNC VS. DUKE GAME THIS WEEKEND. UNC LOOKS LIKE THEY ARE COMING IN HOT! FRANK, WHO DO YOU HAVE WINNING?"

Spoiler alert—no one, not any fan (big or little), will walk away from some fun sports banter.

Sometimes you are unable to conduct enough research to make such remarks, and sometimes the environment is simply not conducive to making small talk. This is when you need to be creative. Be strategic on when you refill your coffee. Has the individual you want to meet stepped outside for a call? Do the same and then consequently end your call at the same time. However, always remember to use your creativity while still respecting boundaries. No one wants to swap business cards in the powder room.

I have attended about eight events with an organization that puts together an executive-level day summit. Typically, about 150 executives attend, along with another fifty individuals who are on their teams. It is a decently large event that promotes discussion and connection. However, even a full-day event can pass a little too quickly when there are only six planned fifteen-minute breaks that enable networking.

At the Atlanta summit for this organization, I had my target prospect list memorized. I met a lot of the leaders on my list and had some fabulously productive conversations. The only person on my list with whom I had not yet connected was Ed, a global executive of Coca-Cola. The day was nearing an end, and I saw Ed step out as the event was wrapping up. I stepped out as well and made my way to the bar, hoping that would be Ed's next move. I've learned after attending many summits and other day-long events that drinks after eight hours of discussion—especially when they are free—are not only welcomed, they are a hot commodity.

Luckily, I was correct, and Ed made his way over to the bar where I was standing "trying to decide" what I was going to order from the all-inclusive bar. Immediately, I turned to Ed and said, "Can I buy you a drink? It's on me!" Using a little passé cocktail reception humor thankfully worked. I continued the conversation by letting Ed know that while I loved Coca-Cola's new "Share a Coke" marketing campaign, I was a little offended that there was no bottle with the name "Betsy" on it. Ed replied with, "Well, we discussed it, but then we realized it was no longer the 1800s." Well-played, Ed.

> "DRIVE YOUR DESTINY AND CREATE YOUR OWN OPPORTUNITIES. FIGURE OUT THE 'WHAT,' THEN WORK ON THE 'HOW.' TRUE, IT IS MUCH EASIER TO SIT BACK AND CHALK UP YOUR FRIENDS'/COLLEAGUES'/ TEAMMATES' OPPORTUNITIES TO LUCK. BUT WHERE DOES DOING SO GET YOU?"

Our light-hearted conversation continued and turned into a deeper business discussion. We stayed in touch after the event. A year later, Ed invited me to Coca-Cola's headquarters to discuss a partnership. I left the meeting with true headway on a partnership and the thoughtful gift of a Coca-Cola bottle with "Betsy" printed on the label.

As I mentioned, there are (thankfully) many leaders who invite others to (metaphorically and physically) sit at the table. Amazing. I imagine these moments as though opportunities are being passed off like batons in a track relay race. It is important to take advantage of these moments, have a strategy, and be prepared, but it is equally important to understand when to sit back and observe.

If you are like me, we, as mid-level professionals, look forward to the ability to engage with leaders and share our insights. But just because you are invited to the table does not mean it is your time to speak out. We've all seen (or maybe, tail between the legs, have even been) that junior-level associate who shares his or her opinion on every single topic whether they were asked to do so or know much about the subject at hand. *Sigh.* It truly is a difficult balance. When to share, when to observe, when to speak out, when to listen. We obviously want to be invited back to the table, so how do we display proper etiquette?

A few ways. It takes acute awareness and attention to nonverbal cues to read the room. If the meeting is asking for opinions or if one of the leaders specifically looks to you to add in your experience, proceed as those bright yellow road signs advise—with caution. Never be too verbose, and do not ever be critical of a given project, program, or initiative (because chances are, someone in the room created, approved, or suggested it). Provide a solution instead of a problem. I like to joke with my team that I am not a problem solver, I am a solution seeker. (You realize now how corny/cliché I can be, right?)

So, you sat at the table. You were silent. Nodded. Agreed. Left. Do not chalk this less-than-desirable interaction up as a lost cause, but instead go directly to your email. Be proactive and type out a recap filled with some insights you observed and ideas for new approaches or next steps. This shows you appreciated the opportunity and that, more importantly, you were engaged and can provide value. Some situations may not always provide you with the entirety of the opportunity, but they can give you that jump start you might need.

If you haven't yet discovered, the overarching theme of this chapter is to drive your destiny and create your own opportunities. Figure out the "what," then work on the "how." True, it is much easier to sit back and chalk up your friends'/colleagues'/teammates' opportunities to luck. But where does doing so get you? Realize you have the potential to do anything you want, as long as you identify the possibilities, use your infallible work ethic, and challenge yourself. Then, your opportunities will not simply be random luck that is imparted on you, but they will be the results of your exertions. Because, like they say—hard workers have all the best luck. Funny how that happens ....

CHAPTER 5

Be Genuine

When I walk into an autograph store (because clearly that is where I hang out), and I pick up a Bears football helmet signed by Jay Cutler, the next thing I do is look for the "authenticity guaranteed" waiver. Better yet, when I walk into a Tory Burch store (that's more like it) and I buy my eighteenth (okay, fine, second, but a girl can dream) handbag, besides considering color, size, design, inside pockets, zippers, and tassels, I look to see if the bag is made of 100% genuine leather.

Being genuine is being authentic, and it is an extremely important attribute at all times. As a society, we have been trained to look for the 100% guarantee in our products and services. However, it is not that easy with people. (But gosh, do I wish it were!) That is just one reason why it is vital to be seen as sincere and authentic in life, especially in the business world. Genuine people are believed to be honest. Honest people are trustworthy. And people do business with those whom they trust.

So, where exactly does that leave the conversations previously mentioned about prior knowledge on an individual's favorite sports team or strategically placing yourself to run into someone? Is doing research on a person to initiate a conversation disingenuous? Some may say so. But I disagree.

Getting the meeting, conducting a conversation, and starting a discussion all amount to just one half of the battle. The second half is what you say and how you say it. I believe your approach when reaching out to individuals will determine your sincerity. No one can criticize someone for doing their due diligence—even if that means researching a person's work and educational background. It is how one uses this information that determines the authenticity behind it. After you make initial contact and land another meeting, be honest in the follow-up conversations and work to develop your connection into a more lasting and meaningful relationship. Nothing is more detrimental to a relationship than a "one and done" mentality— you know, the let's-have-one-conversation-and-then-I-am-done-talking-to-you-goodbye approach.

Relationships, no matter from where or how they are derived, should be looked at as investments. Investments for your business, your personal brand, your professional career, and your success. As with all investments, the more you put in, the more you get on your return. Relationships establish likability and trust. You wouldn't be in a relationship, no matter a friend, boyfriend, girlfriend, or partner, with someone you didn't like or trust.

So, you get the meeting—how do you invest and create genuine likability? For me, I use compliments, which sounds easier than it actually is. Do not simply walk in and compliment the business, the office, an outfit, an organization's mission or values, etc. Do your research.

> "PEOPLE CAN SEE THROUGH A
> FAKE CONVERSATION. DON'T LET
> YOURSELF COME OFF AS DISINGENUOUS.
> LET YOUR TRUE IDENTITY SHINE
> THROUGH THE CONVERSATION."

I have found people are much more open to discussion when a conversation begins on a positive note or with a compliment. Alternatively, I have seen people shut down when someone has walked into a meeting, sat down, and started asking a company about its problems. No one likes to admit to flaws, or worse, to discuss them with near-strangers or even old acquaintances. Would you walk into a new friend's home and immediately ask them if they had leaks, good insulation, electrical problems, or asbestos, without maybe first pointing out how nice the windows are or what a great part of town the house is in? I hope is the answer here is a resounding "NO!"

And as silly as that sounds, I have seen people walk into business meetings, hoping to make the company a client and start by telling its employees how he or she can solve X problem with their Y solution which usually always ends with the (no longer) potential client telling them to Z-I-P their lips. I mean because honestly, would you walk into a first date and tell the person, "You are a loner and probably need to get married so I will be your fiancé to solve this"? Um, LOL, bye.

I have learned a compliment usually leads to additional conversation, which can uncover some other useful information like details or event imperfections. "I love your sweater! Is it Louis Vuitton?" might lead to the response, "Oh, this old thing? Thanks! I got it at Nordstrom—and it was on sale!" (Personally, I love people who share coveted fashion secrets.) And sometimes those secrets lead to other hidden secrets. You might tell your friend in all honesty, "Dinner was amazing. I am sure you worked away in the kitchen for hours!" And she might respond with, "Thanks! It was super easy. It was only five ingredients and took me less than thirty minutes. I'll give you the recipe!" Which is exactly how I got my sister-in-law Mary's white bean chili recipe. (It really is so good—let me know if you want it, and trust me, you need it.)

Let's put this notion to life. While leading the national expansion for the IT company, I would often meet with local individuals in hopes of signing them on as clients. The company provided various IT solutions, including building out website platforms. When meeting with prospects in such regards, I would first find something that truly stood out about their website. I would begin the conversation with how I genuinely liked the feature and why I found it to be efficacious. This technique created a bond of likability and showed the individual or individuals with whom I was working that I had done my research prior to the meeting. Remember, often times when you provide a compliment, people are more likely to uncover their secrets, maybe even bring up their hidden flaws or challenges. For me, complimenting a side panel on a website resulted in uncovering the real issues the company was having with said website. Whatever you say, be honest—people can see through disingenuity. So please, always make the compliment real (resisting urge to quote *Mean Girls* here).

Being genuine is being the most authentic form of yourself. It is easy to lose a sense of sincerity, particularly when you are in a sales role. People can see through a fake conversation. Don't let yourself come off as disingenuous. Let your true identity shine through the conversation. Remember earlier when I spoke about personifying yourself? This vital technique comes into play once again.

When I am at a large event, whether it be a cocktail reception or a day summit, I want people to see through my job/sales pitch/networking scheme to see my personality. I'll be the first person to capitalize on a Cubs baseball comment, turning the conversation from the mundane details of work into one of sports, hopefully creating team camaraderie. There is always an opportunity to talk business once you've established a connection or, better yet, a relationship with someone. Create the relationship on a shared connection, instilling trust and enabling your personality to show. It's not a coincidence that people tend to work more often with others they like.

⌒⌒

I had a mentor once who had a simply contagious energy. This woman was charming and seemed to be able to land any sale. As I sat in meetings, watching my mentor talk to clients, I observed how she exuded this same kind of energy to the people around us. But then I also began to notice something else.

While this person truly appeared to be positive and full of life, her behavior was not authentic. Every meeting I witnessed was executed in an overwhelmingly excited manner. True, in the beginning, her demeanor *was* contagious. Prospective clients nodded and agreed with every word, and like a bad case of the flu, they caught the energy. However, as a second or third meeting progressed, the exciting promises my mentor had made proved to be empty. And while the energy was still high, the morale was now low. This was a huge realization for me. I noticed this woman, my role model, was not entirely straightforward in her responses in order to continue a sale in a positive manner and that her behavior, in turn, ultimately felt disingenuous.

In the beginning, I saw a lot of myself in this mentor, the energy, determination, and positive attitude. I began to focus immensely on my interactions with others. While being authentic to myself, I was insistent on being realistic to the situation at hand and being 100% honest. I hope my mentor never meant to intentionally deceive an individual or lie about her own or the company's capabilities. Maybe the desire to fill the need, play the right character, or provide the answer she thought the client wanted to hear had fogged her authentic self. However, from that moment on, I challenged myself to never do the same.

Let your personality shine, but not in a way that compromises promises.

⌒⌒

I am a lot. I don't really know how else to say it, so I will just go with that and let you decipher it from there. But sure, I'll help. I am loud, opinionated, and easily excitable. But I am also, (though most miss this due to my overwhelming personality), introspective, reflective, and empathetic.

One time at a party, I was (maybe overly) excited to see old friends. I saw someone no one knew standing alone (because isn't that the worst?) and wanted to help her feel included. I probably went overkill when I bopped (literally) over to her, started talking about most likely everything, and invited her into the conversation. Later, I found out she told her husband I was overbearing (in today's words: *extra*). Face = bright red.

I get it. I'm what my friends (lovingly?) call animated. I don't always know how to fully control the volume of my voice or my squeal of a reaction when I am excited. But I'm working on it. I have learned this is in fact me, but while I am reacting authentically, others might easily observe my behavior as disingenuous. And I can't blame them for that. Just as much as you need to be your true self, I have learned that others need to be so too. And when you step into their world (inviting yourself into a conversation) or walk into the work force (with etiquette and culture), sometimes your authentic self needs to be leveled.

While I am a strong advocate for giving yourself permission to live a big life and never dimming your shine for someone else, I am also continuously learning to understand the comfort zones of others and how people might perceive certain interactions. While I am unapologetically me, I am still working on how to be both who I am and understanding how others discern that.

One day, I was at yet another coffee meeting, sitting with yet another business leader. Holding their full attention, I started my meeting as I usually did by asking about this person's career path. As this woman sat across the table from me, she shared her perfectly rehearsed pitch about her first job, her big break, and her current opportunities. Then she stopped and told me something that left me absolutely shook, followed by some powerful advice.

"I have not hit my goals in three quarters. And it is not from a lack of effort," she said. "I am not on track to hit them yet again. But that does not mean I am giving up. I am struggling, and it's hard."

After she told me that, I sat there in a mixture of shock and confusion. First off, why was she telling me this? Secondly, I thought she was supposed to be a successful, put-together, flawless businesswoman. Third, how on Earth was I to respond? Luckily, I didn't have to because she spoke again.

"I have learned that in order to get to know someone in the most genuine form, you need to tell that person something personal about yourself. Let yourself be vulnerable." She continued, "When you do this, the individual can see you are serious about the conversation, you are real and that we, especially as women, need each other to succeed. By allowing yourself to be vulnerable, you are opening yourself up to this person and trusting them, which will hopefully encourage them to do the same."

This was such brilliant advice. Before this meeting, I would have done anything to hide my failings and cover up my mistakes—especially when in the company of people I wanted to impress. However, I have since seen how the conversation takes a whole different spin when I allow myself to open up.

Now, don't take this suggestion and go into every interview and meeting revealing all the times you crashed and burned and then expect great results. However, I have conducted multiple business meetings since then where I have confided in the individual. If a client and I were speaking about a project, I would tell them about my positive experience with similar assignments. Then, I would pull a game changer and talk about a situation where the task at hand went a little differently than intended. I would emphasize what lessons I learned from that outcome, which would ideally show my abilities to adapt and grow.

Opening up to others about my shortcomings provided me with so many things. I learned I was not alone. Far too often, people are able to hide behind a screen, whether it be an Instagram profile, an annual report, or a private company earnings report; these kinds of things don't show everything. We are able to cover our bruises and hide our battle wounds. But sometimes, simply by sharing horror stories, especially when we're in them, we find someone who is either lying in the trenches with us or has been there before and can help us crawl out.

I've realized most people like to sing their own praises—especially when there is a competitive edge in doing so. Challenge yourself to do what others will not. Call out your failures. Disclosing those unfortunate times when you fell short of success may not be the easiest task. Learn how to be comfortable with your mistakes and determine how they have provided you with a platform to become better at your job. It is a known fact: everyone makes mistakes. Allow yourself to make light of the mistakes you have made in a positive way so they are seen as opportunities that enabled lessons.

As your clients, prospects, partners, and colleagues begin to learn more about you—positive and negative (or better yet, negative turned positive)—they begin to see you as your authentic self. One positive retrospective outcome from being genuine is that people will trust you. And when people trust what you say, they will trust what you do and, most importantly, what you say you will do. They believe you and, in turn, they believe *in* you. Being genuine eliminates the need to make excuses.

Excuses are one of the biggest deterrents from being genuine. I have had plenty of meetings where (I am ashamed to admit) I was late. I have had some of the best excuses around—my power went off and thus shut down my alarm clock; my neighbor blocked in my car; I got hit by a deer (yes, the deer hit me!). Were these excuses real? Sure. Does that matter? No. Because despite what your reason is for missing a meeting, being late to a call, or forgetting a report, the only thing the other person hears is one overwhelming, deafening statement: this meeting/report/call was not important enough to you to be on time. And when someone thinks that, the trust is lost.

Walking into a meeting anything other than five minutes early is slightly (if not entirely) embarrassing. This embarrassment grows exponentially greater as not being early turns into being late. One time in particular, I was meeting with a business leader whom I respect. I left later than I should have and did not account for traffic. Lo and behold, traffic was worse than usual, and my arrival time slowly turned from being fifteen minutes early to fifteen minutes late.

> "MOST PEOPLE LIKE TO SING THEIR OWN PRAISES—ESPECIALLY WHEN THERE IS A COMPETITIVE EDGE IN DOING SO. CHALLENGE YOURSELF TO DO WHAT OTHERS WILL NOT. CALL OUT YOUR FAILURES."

I sent my mentor a message, letting him know I was in fact on my way, but I would be late. Upon arriving (with my tail between my legs, mortified), I gave a sincere apology, stating I had no excuse and it was my fault that I greatly underestimated the drive. Our meeting went on and we had a great discussion. I followed up with a hand-written card to the business leader. In my card, I thanked him for the meeting, apologized for my tardiness, attached a gift card for a cup of coffee, and stated I would love to meet again. Two weeks later, the company that business leader represented signed on as a client.

Things happen; people are late, meetings are forgotten, mistakes are made. Do not allow yourself to use an excuse—real or fictitious—as a crutch. Take the blame. People tend to be understanding and are a lot more receptive when you take ownership of the situation instead of playing the victim. (But seriously—that deer *did* hit me.)

Throughout my different roles in different companies, I have seen one strong attribute in myself that has helped to solidify my genuineness. That attribute is passion. No one can doubt a person who cares so much about a subject their eyes light up, they talk a little (but not too much) faster, and they become outwardly excited. Passion exudes sincerity. So, be passionate about your work, job, assignment, role, project.

What happens when it's hard to find that passion? Do your best to change your circumstances. If you cannot change them, change the way you think about them.

You know what I hate? Entering data. But because of the data I have entered, I have been able to review some pretty important details from conversations I've had. These specifics later helped me to build strong relationships. So, I enter data. This boring task surely does not make my eyes glow gold with passion, but it is only a small aspect of my job. I try to couple it with things I do enjoy, such as listening to the newest Beyoncé album or sipping my grande triple hot pumpkin spice latte (hold the basic). The essential part of my job is working with others, talking with others, connecting with others. And that is what I love most. That is where my true passion lies. And while the data entry is undoubtedly boring and mundane, it ultimately enables me to be better at my job. When you are struggling to find or reconnect with whatever you feel most passionate about, try to remember other facets of your job or previous moments in your professional life that can give you inspiration and motivation.

> "THERE MAY BE FEAR IN BEING YOUR AUTHENTIC SELF, AND REGARDLESS OF WHO YOU ARE (OR WHO YOU PRETEND YOU ARE), SOME PEOPLE WILL ALWAYS FIND A PROBLEM WITH IT. YOU CAN NEVER PLEASE EVERYONE, SO AT THE RISK OF SOUNDING EXTREMELY CLICHÉ: BE YOU."

Let's be honest: sometimes it is hard to be your genuine, authentic self. The line separating work and life went from ever-present to hardly existent. It's okay to be feminine! It's okay to be bossy, aggressive, sassy, direct. Never trade in your authenticity for approval. There may be fear in being your authentic self, and regardless of who you are (or who you pretend you are), some people will always find a problem with it. You can never please everyone, so at the risk of sounding extremely cliché: be you.

⚬⚬⚬

It's time to self-reflect. Yes, on yourself! You will find parts of your identity that are strong assets in the boardroom, uncover others that may need a little development, and discover even more traits you unfortunately don't (yet) have but hope to cultivate. Allow yourself to be transparent, and being genuine will come naturally. Be just as open with your failures as you are with your successes. Let others see your passion through your work. Bring your personal qualities to your role. And most importantly, be consistent. Being your authentic self means you will be unapologetically you, in your best form, enabling yourself to grow, develop, and learn. Repeat that: best form. Mirror what you admire.

I am not always the person I want to be, but I'm trying. I am a work in progress. And while I am still growing and learning, I am (like it or not) unapologetically Betsy Mack, sometimes too loud, somewhat bossy, silly, slightly overbearing, direct—but always 100% authentic and genuine. I am still working on development and being my best version, but I am me.

CHAPTER 6

Make Your Net Work

We've all heard it (right?): your network is your net worth. And if that's the case, cast that net and put it to work.

Have you ever had a dear, but very under-qualified friend receive a job because they "knew someone who worked there"? Was it luck? No; it was that friend's network. Hello truth, we meet again.

While on the winding road of defining your work ethic, surround yourself with fellow doers and achievers. This is pivotal—not only to help yourself better learn various skills, but to align yourself with individuals who share similar values.

Motivational speaker Jim Rohn famously said, "we are the average of the five people we spend the most time with." Whether there is any concrete evidence behind this statement remains to be determined. Still, I am sure most people can find some truth within it. So, choose your company wisely. These people are your influencers, your mentors, your mentees, your supporters.

Look at your network as your circle of influence. Your network is an all-encompassing web of individuals with whom you meet, work, and connect. The larger the network, the larger—and more entwined—the web becomes. I love using the analogy of a web when describing a network because it truly tends to become one, a complex system of interconnected, intricate threads with you in the middle.

The more involved I became in the community, the smaller the community became. When I was at United Way, in my first office in the small town of Granite City, I was expected to attend every community event, including the opening of the town's first movie theater with a ribbon-cutting ceremony performed by the mayor. (Did I mention it was a small town?) Attending events with the mayor, local company presidents, general managers, and town leaders was intimidating at first. But one by one, I was able to connect with some of these individuals. And better yet, I learned their stories, their backgrounds. While everyone in Granite City was deeply connected (small town, remember?), they all had relationships outside of the area as well.

As I moved out of the Granite City office and into United Way's downtown St. Louis headquarters, I continued to meet more people. However, I made it a goal to stay in touch with the people I had worked with in my previous role. I find it of the utmost value to continue to keep in touch with those who have helped me to achieve success. At United Way, an entire board of people helped me to directly hit and surpass my fundraising goal. It is not lost on me that without them, I would not have succeeded.

When you are trying to move up in your career or move across the area, industry, or sector from which you came, how on Earth are you supposed to keep in touch with everyone? It certainly is not easy. I try and stay in touch with my key group of contacts quarterly. I keep an Excel spreadsheet (yes—I am just *that* tech savvy) of individuals with whom I have connected as well as with whom I hope to connect. I label each individual in my ever-growing list of categories of young leaders, the metropolitan area in which they are located, at what level they work, whether they are close acquaintances of mine or others I know well, and people I have identified as potential mentors. Try starting such a list yourself, or if you already have one, challenge yourself to add five, twenty-five, fifty new names by a specific date.

As mentioned, I try to connect with these individuals at least quarterly. I usually reach out through email in a mail-merge type of message. Yes, one of those "this looks like a personal message, but really you're one of two hundred ... but let's pretend you can't tell because this looks pretty individualistic" platforms.

Obviously, I send the standard holiday message around Thanksgiving. The end of January, I find, is the best month for outreach in terms of response rate. Life has finally slowed down for most people—but business around this time of the year is increasing to warp speed. I reach out to ask about the holiday season (because just enough time has passed now for people to reminisce on the happy moments, having forgotten that Aunt June vacuumed up your cat and Grandpa Earl sat on the pumpkin pie) and ask how business is going. Because let's be honest—with every connection, outreach, conversation, there is the hope of some opportunity, be it new business, a potential client, a future mentor, a connection, ally, or friend. My two other strategic contact initiatives come prior to Memorial Day—when I ask about summer plans—and again post Labor Day, when I close the seasonal loop by asking how the summer passed.

I will admit my methodology certainly has flaws: details are not all tracked in a neat little CRM box, messages bounce back, and sometimes responses all flood back simultaneously. I know there are amazing platforms you can buy to do this kind of large-scale email outreach for you now. But this strategy works for me. It has been an evolving approach with one goal in mind: to stay in touch with my network. And that goal has been mostly achieved.

> "MAKE USE OF YOUR NETWORK IN A
> WAY THAT BENEFITS THOSE INDIVIDUALS
> AS MUCH AS IT BENEFITS YOU."

So, you have a network. Now what? Send empty and meaningless emails and/ or letters? Please, no. *Utilize these contacts.* However, do not get this message confused with me saying "use them." Exploiting your network is the fastest way to lose contact. Instead, make use of your network in a way that benefits those individuals as much as it benefits you. Do you have a question and need advice? Do you have an extra ticket to an event? Do you have an open board seat? Extending favors to others is the best way for people to extend favors to you.

Throughout my professional roles, I have been fortunate to attend a lot of community events. And at these luncheons, cocktail receptions, and galas, my company would usually purchase a full table. I loved having the challenge—better yet, the opportunity—to fill a table for a fun event. People love being invited, no matter what the occasion.

For three years straight, I attended the Regional Business Alliance Council Annual Meeting in Charlotte. It has always been one of my favorite community events as it fills up with more than 500 business executives and honors a group of fabulously successful leaders. One year I had a table for ten to fill. I reached out to a number of people in my network. The best part about the table of individuals who attended was the diversity in the group. All of the attendees I had invited were from different parts of my career path. However, as always, I had a strategy. I invited those with whom I wanted to reconnect, better connect, or whom I wanted to connect to each other. Because who doesn't love when networking events become more about reunions than new meetings?

Connecting your network is a great approach that has multiple benefits. When you connect other people, the base of their relationships is associated with you as you continue to entwine and expand your network. Some of my greatest colleagues and friends have been formed through introductions. I always find it to be such a compliment when someone tells me I have to meet his or her [insert business partner, colleague, mentor, boss here].

Seth, the mentor I mentioned in a previous chapter, was the president of the company I worked for at the time. At one of our first meetings, he suggested I get to know one particular extremely talented young professional also at the company. Seth said we had similar work ethics and we would both benefit from a conversation. And so, I reached out and met Maura.

Maura and I were both young enough in our careers then to want growth, but experienced enough to know growth would come through time, effort, and results. We had a great talk and learned a lot from each other and from the fact our career paths were different, despite having similar aspirations.

As I continued to meet other women in the business community who had parallel ambitions to mine, I set up additional meetings to hear about them and their careers in hopes of learning more. Learning more about what, exactly? I was not completely certain. I just knew I wanted to understand their stories and absorb their insights and discover other potential paths on the ever-winding journey to success. While filling just about every morning with one-on-one, similarly focused discussions was extremely enlightening, it was not conducive to my time management. Thus, I created an informal, unnamed women's young professional group.

The ladies in the group were all like-minded, focused, and determined yet diverse in industry, background, and experience. We met monthly at Starbucks, discussing topics such as women leaders, the term "young professionals," mentors, and organizations with which to affiliate. I first invited twelve ladies, but the group mostly consisted of six core members. Why these ladies? Why this core? No real reason. The group continued to expand any time I met other eager women. With scheduling conflicts or other obligations and priorities, we always managed to be a smaller group. And to be honest, being smaller was more conducive to having productive and engaging conversations.

The discussions were never the same and some were more beneficial than others. But each one provided value. At one meeting in particular, we discussed an individual work issue one of the members was dealing with. At another get together, we dove head-first into actionable ways to find a mentor, with each person leaving with the homework of introducing a fellow member to a prospective mentor. One of the key concepts that became immediately clear was we were all passionate about our careers. And as I stated before, one cannot doubt or question a person's passion.

As an outgoing, civic-focused individual, I always try to be not only involved, but also invested in my community. I want to plant roots and establish myself. And my network has been a key factor in enabling my roots to not only grow, but flourish.

Networking events can be tedious. Far too well, I know the mundane feeling of walking into yet another crowded room, in those uncomfortable but oh-so-cute Jessica Simpson heels, looking for unfamiliar faces with notable name tags and shaking their hands. Still, I am proof that it pays off. Despite the number of events you attend, walking into a room of strangers is intimidating. Don't look at it as daunting, but as an opportunity. You have a blank canvas in front of you; armed with a set of fresh brushes, you are ready to paint whatever you want. Attending the multiple Granite City events taught me that the more involved in the community I was, the smaller that community became. I started to recognize people, and, better yet, they started to recognize me.

Let's be honest. Though it is easier to seek out a familiar face, most people who attend networking events are prepared and hoping to meet new people. Remembering this fact makes it easier to approach fellow event attendees. I have learned the easiest way to start a conversation is through a compliment followed by a question or statement that prompts a response, such as: "I love your shoes! Please tell me they are more comfortable than mine." Or just call yourself out: "What a great turnout. Are all events this well-attended? This is my first time at this speaker series." Regardless of your approach, including an opportunity for the other person to engage with you is critical, because nothing is worse than getting a nod or an "uh huh" response to the thought-out statement you had to give yourself a pep talk to give.

Right, so networking events may not be your thing. That's fine. What about other avenues? I also touched on board roles and my involvement in some. This is where I gained a few mentors as noted in Chapter Three. A board is a great opportunity to truly expand your network across multiple facets—including age, industry, and sometimes geographic area.

Okay, great, I'm in, you're thinking. Is this another sign-up sheet getting passed around that I just so happened to miss? Nope. It takes outreach and a plan. There are so many questions you need to ask yourself when looking to join a board. Did anyone else ever read *Cosmopolitan* growing up? Remember those quizzes that took you on a little journey down the page to correctly categorize you based off your responses? (If you are shaking your head, just advance forward to the end of this paragraph. But if you are nodding like, "Yes, girl!" then, hello! We are back circa 2002!)

Let's begin:

1. WHY ARE YOU JOINING A BOARD?
2. TO GAIN BOARD EXPERIENCE/BUILD YOUR RESUME: ADVANCE TO OPTION 1
3. TO LEARN A NEW SKILL: IDENTIFY THAT SKILL AND ADVANCE TO OPTION 2
4. TO MEET PEOPLE IN THE MEDICAL INDUSTRY: ADVANCE TO OPTION 3

OPTION 1:
That's great! You have to start somewhere, right? Find something about which you're passionate about where you can learn more and enjoy it while you serve.

OPTION 2:
First, identify this skill, whether it is accounting, fundraising, event planning, etc. Define what it is you want to gain from your board seat. It is your time you're volunteering (can we say "free labor"?). Make it worthwhile. Does this skill have to directly relate to your current line of work? NO. If you are in a finance job and you love event planning—not enough to quit and become a full-time wedding planner, but just enough to miss it—use your board seat as your outlet. It is quite literally a win-win. You are able to utilize (and strengthen) this skill set, and a board is able to leverage that with their low overhead and cost-saving abilities. So, you defined it, great. Now find a nonprofit that needs it.

OPTION 3:
Okay, so back to the ol' network. Maybe you are not quite this specific with the types of individuals you want to meet by industry. However, if you are in medical device sales and focusing on a targeted group, I sure hope you are focused on meeting others in the medical industry. But for those of us who are not, be sure to identify the type of people you want to meet—meaning young professionals, religion-focused groups, politically aligned groups, the LGBTQ community,

etc. Most boards do a great job of identifying a mix of leaders to engage with, from different backgrounds, industries, levels. Make sure that while boards are able to have a few defining factors to them (industry specific/LGBTQ-focused/ geographically located, etc.), make sure there are more factors diversifying them. A board comprised of the same people with the same backgrounds, viewpoints, beliefs, upbringings, career level, values, nail color, shoe sizes, <enter every single descriptor here>, will most likely not bring about any differentiating, new ideas, thus not really helping with that network expansion, huh?

And now zooming back out.

For those who think networking is only done at business events, I am about to blow your mind. I have met business colleagues while at yoga, getting ice cream, walking through the park, and (obviously) at my second home (Starbucks). I am, admittedly, that embarrassing friend who will walk into a place and start a conversation with the person standing next to me. One of my friends likes to remind me I have never met a stranger. Best compliment ever.

Once, while sitting on my yoga mat, stretching before class, I started a conversation with the lady next to me by asking her where she had gotten her yoga pants. Seriously, they were hot pink, gray, had mesh cut outs and were quite fabulous—I needed them. Turns out, Lauren had purchased the Lululemon-looking tights at a fraction of the cost from Forever 21 (thank you for being fab and helping me look like I spend millions). She thanked me for the compliment, stating she was glad they at least looked expensive because she was actually in between jobs and didn't want to give off that impression. And just like that, my thoughts went into overdrive, and my networking lightbulb illuminated at 250 watts.

Lauren and I went for a coffee after class and talked for hours. I learned about her skill set and what she was hoping for in her next job. She walked away with new contacts to reach out to at local nonprofit agencies, and I walked away with a new colleague and friend.

The key thing I have learned from networking is to look at everyone as a prospect. Never say no to someone. Give them the opportunity to learn about your company and the value proposition you offer. A vital lesson I learned from my fundraising days is that the number one reason people don't give to your cause or partner with your organization is they simply were not asked to do so. If my previous Greek mythology lesson about Mentor taught you nothing earlier, then I hope this reference to the Oracle of Delphi will redeem me: Leave no stone unturned.

I somehow became a regular at a café in Charlotte called Not Just Coffee. "The usual?" the waitress asked me one sunny morning, to which a nearby customer responded with a joke, "Wait, I didn't see that on the menu." Face meet palm. I get it—I come here a lot.

The gentleman and I ended up having a short but sweet conversation, exchanged business cards, and carried on with our days. We partook in our due diligence of a follow-up "nice to meet you" email and went our separate ways. A few weeks later, I was on a local news outlet promoting an event I was co-chairing. Turns out my lunch friend was watching, was interested in the event, reached out to congratulate my success, and purchased two tickets for himself and his wife. As theologian and author John of Salisbury said, standing on the shoulders of giants does not make us superior, it only greatens our stature. Your network is your net worth. By definition, net worth is the total assets minus the total outside liabilities. Look at negative people, situations, and experiences as liabilities and eliminate them. Now go surround yourself with those who raise you up. Create a network of individuals who inspire you. These people are the assets who will add value to your net worth. And so, my adventures continue. New places, new people, new stories. I sure don't know everyone, nor do I know their stories, but I want to. And I want people to want to know mine. And I hope you feel the same about your own stories. Strive to be a person worth meeting, a person worth adding to someone's network. And once you have your network, be sure to make your own net work.

CHAPTER 7

Public Image and Personal Brand

Walking through the grocery store, with a list in hand, I usually know what I am looking for. And when I reach toward the shelf with about six different brands staring back at me, it may seem like I have a lot of options. But to me, the choices are simple: Coca-Cola for my diet soda, Kraft for my cheese, Prairie Farms Dairy for my milk.

I am sure many other people are the same way. And it is because of a simple, recognized reason: brand loyalty. It is so intriguing to me when a company has built a reputation so strong it embodies its values and mission. Most companies have brands—positive or negative—that are created through experiences, interactions, and situations with their customers. It is interesting to think and imperative to realize that like companies, individuals also have brands. A personal brand is the ongoing process of defining yourself and establishing a reputation. A personal brand is not a simple process of creating an image; rather, it is a continual progression.

Commoditization is usually synonymous with devaluation. When one commoditizes, one implies the companies, brands, or services being discussed are the same. And when you do that, it eliminates the individual value proposition that the item, person, place, or situation offers and focuses on the most eminent factor, which is usually the price, availability, or proximity.

Think about it. If your significant other told you he needed flowers for a centerpiece and did not care about the type, what would you do? You are not looking at flowers as individual items, thinking about different colors or types. You are going to purchase the flowers based on other factors, such as which source is the closest, most convenient, or cheapest. Lilies at Lowe's for $5.99? Done. Because individual flowers have been commoditized, you would use one unifying factor to make your decision. And this unifying factor is usually one that does not do the individual product or service justice.

Because of this concept, creating a personal brand is imperative. View it as your value proposition that defines who you are and sets you apart from the other two-legged, two-eyed humans around you. By creating a personal brand, you are able to create your own defining factor, instead of letting others decide on a unifying factor that devalues you.

Personal branding is a full-time commitment to the journey of defining yourself. I believe there are four aspects that help to create your personal brand:

1. THE PEOPLE WITH WHOM YOU INTERACT,
2. THE ORGANIZATIONS WITH WHICH YOU AFFILIATE,
3. THE COMPANIES YOU REPRESENT,
4. THE APPEARANCE YOU PROVIDE.

Your personal brand is an important aspect of yourself that you should value. Many people do not place a lot of emphasis on their own brand, and that may be just fine. However, I assure you, those who do will benefit immensely because your brand is your reputation, your identity, and your distinctive characteristics that can set you apart (and enable you to shine) within a group, crowd, or company and among competitors.

The people with whom you interact have a large impact on your personal brand. For better or for worse, the company you keep can start to define who you are and how you are perceived. Remember Jim Rohn's philosophy from Chapter Six? You are the average of the five people with whom you spend the most time.

Large events can provide great ways to network, but they can also be overwhelming. When walking into a room full of people, how often do you look for someone you know? Finally, from across the room, you spot a friend from what seems like a lifetime ago. Making your way over to this person, he or she graciously introduces you to another friend. How many of you would automatically assimilate this new stranger to have the same characteristics as your long-lost friend? Values, character traits, and work ethic when unknown are usually assumed to be similar if not the same as the individual with whom you are interacting. Why? Because this is your brain's way of filling in the gaps. This is where assumptions come from. You are trying to make sense of a situation and insert facts where there are blanks. Is this practice accurate? Probably not. But it happens, so we need to be aware.

> "PERSONAL BRANDING IS A
> FULL-TIME COMMITMENT TO THE
> JOURNEY OF DEFINING YOURSELF."

When I worked at United Way alongside my mentor and friend Marilyn, I learned how true it is that we assimilate others' characteristics when we first meet them. I believe I have a strong work ethic and positive values upon which I base my career. As I learned more about Marilyn, I continued to be impressed with her attributes. Whenever Marilyn and I were out in the community, she would introduce me to many of her friends and colleagues. Because of Marilyn's reputation in the business world, people welcomed me in and began to put faith in my skills. Having Marilyn's endorsement was seen as confirmation that I too had a strong work ethic, which in turn helped to build on my personal brand.

Consequently, because I was working so closely with Marilyn and sometimes speaking on her behalf, I had an obligation to uphold her pristine reputation. The ever-so-popular phrase says it best: "You are the company you keep." While out in the community, I see a lot of truth this statement. Just as with my women's young professional group, like minds are attracted to each other. The network you build, which we just discussed in great lengths, should build you up in return and be an asset to not only your daily life but also your brand.

Just as the people with whom you interact influence your brand, so too do the organizations you represent, or for which you work or volunteer. Be strategic when choosing the organizations and causes you support. While you are using an organization to network, others may be using the organization to understand you.

While working at United Way, there were some controversial issues around The Boys Scouts of America. The Boy Scouts had a few programs that the United Way of Greater St. Louis funded. The organization was undergoing some strategic planning that centered its focus on homosexuality. While United Way of Greater St. Louis took a neutral stance on the subject, the community did not. Some people believed

United Way had taken sides on the subject matter. Our senior vice president kept us well-versed on how to stay politically correct and ensure our unbiased position led us to be neither for nor against the issue.

The importance of understanding an organization's mission statement and core values is crucial. When you begin to volunteer with an organization, no matter what level, you align yourself with their ethics. As an organization grows and endures leadership turnover, values evolve. As change happens, it is perfectly acceptable to reevaluate your relationship to these values and walk away if need be.

I was involved with a local nonprofit for which I volunteered my time as a board member. I believed fully in their mission and respected their approach. After a year on the board, the organization began to move toward different initiatives. While I still supported the objectives, I no longer felt the nonprofit was helping the need in the community I was so passionate about. I tried to leverage my board role to influence a change; however, top leaders were adamant on the new direction. After a respectful conversation, we decided to part ways.

I find this situation to be extremely enlightening. It confirms the notion that evolution is an organic process apparent in life, business, and organizations. Most things—people, animals, companies—are not the same when looking from start to finish. As times change, as situations occur, as demands are placed, aspects change. I felt confident with the decision to move forward and begin working with a different organization that better aligned with my values. I realized my time and effort would not help the organization to benefit in their new initiative, so it was the best decision for both parties.

Just as the organizations with which you volunteer are important, so is the company where you work. Research your company from every single angle. Look at it from every different side: as an investor, a client, a partner, an employee, a volunteer, a parent. The more aspects you obtain, the better you can understand the company. As you take on the identity of the company employee, you take on every interaction someone has had before you. So, if the company is known for having poor communication, you now do as well.

In the same light, learn how to help ensure a positive reputation for the company. It affects your personal brand just as much as it reiterates the company's brand. Strong company brands do not simply just appear. They are the outcome of marketing efforts and positive interactions.

In St. Louis, United Way has a fabulous reputation. The organization has top leadership support from all of the local Fortune 500 companies as well as about 2,500 other local industries. United Way of Greater St. Louis has been endorsed personally from countless leaders and has the reputation of "running like a well-oiled machine."

When out in the community, I loved telling people I worked for United Way. I wore this fact like a badge of honor. And when people asked where I worked, I loved when their response would reveal that they too supported the organization and all of its great work for the area. Upon leaving the organization, I was honored to still be involved as a Women's Leadership Society Cabinet Member.

When I worked in Dallas for a short period of time, I became involved on the board with United Way locally. They also had a fabulous reputation with which I was more than happy to associate. After moving to Charlotte, I yet again reached out to United Way to plant my roots.

In Charlotte, I quickly learned United Way did not hold the same flawless reputation of an upstanding organization as it did in St. Louis and Dallas. Unfortunately, there was a situation with a previous executive that had occurred years (and years) ago. Despite the time that had passed, the residents of Charlotte had not yet forgotten or forgiven the damaging event. Whereas I had received looks of gratitude for my association with United Way in St. Louis, in Charlotte, my involvement received looks of skepticism.

Despite the questionable local reputation, I was and continue to be confident in the national reputation. After moving to Charlotte, I met Tina, who at the time was one of the Senior VPs at the local affiliate, and felt thankful for her energy, passion, and objectives. As she led the United Way of the Central Carolinas toward a new initiative of engaging the community and involving local business leaders, I was thankful to be included. Because as quickly as a reputation can be tarnished, the tide can turn, new leaders can take over, and a fresh foundation will appear upon which to build a new brand.

⚬≈⚬

The first three aspects we've discussed in this chapter are all third-party factors that influence your personal brand. However, the most important aspect regarding your brand is how you present yourself. The presentation is all-encompassing, across multiple platforms. It is the tone you use, the way you dress, the actions you take, how you utilize social media outlets, the words you speak, and how you introduce yourself, among other factors.

When reaching out or setting up any type of meeting, the first thing I do is search Google for the person with whom I am to meet. I never walk into a meeting blindly. I like to know who I am looking for by finding a picture, and I like to understand a small bit about this person's background from any online profiles. In a digital world, being aware of what you put out into cyberspace is imperative. With tools like online search engines and platforms that allow us to type our every thought, what happens in Vegas no longer stays there.

Thankfully, I have not fallen victim to a social media scandal that has taken over my career. But I have felt the effects of small-minded people who have tried to sabotage me through fake pictures and false profiles. Not to validate the situation, but minor instances have occurred where individuals have taken my pictures and used them in ways I did not approve. If I have learned anything from those experiences, it is to never give people the ammunition to shoot you. Not that I am suggesting we all hide our pictures and profiles and live in private mode; some jobs do not allow for that, especially those that are in a public-facing role. Simply stated: do not subject yourself to inappropriate pictures or to controversial statements. Too many times we hear someone posted a comment in rage, only to now have it tarnish his or her reputation. Above all, live in a way that if someone were to inflict such actions onto you/your image/your brand, others simply would not believe it or know it to not, in any way, be true.

Our world has changed from one where people were able to separate work life and personal life to one of blurred lines. Someone once told me there is no longer a work-life balance, that it is actually a work-life blend. I try very hard to create my public and personal images to be ones of utmost respect, but also of transparency. I want the Betsy who people see in the boardroom to be similar to the Betsy they see at the bar. Obviously, different environments call for different tones; however, I want my identity, personality, and character to be constant. I want my personality to shine through in a light in which I am proud to be seen. Throughout any interaction, occasion, or situation, I want my values to remain consistent and translucent. And I challenge you to do the same.

CHAPTER 8

Time

Like most, I live off of my calendar. And not a cute little Kate Spade notebook like my sister, Amy, so gracefully uses. My calendar is virtual, synced to my phone, computer, tablet, and somewhere up in the cloud. My schedule is packed, complex, and ever-changing. Dinging iPhone alerts and fifteen-minute reminder queues guide my days. In a world where we are constantly on the move, how do we ensure we productively capture the information we need to obtain, and absorb the thoughts we need to keep, instead of just floating aimlessly from meeting to meeting?

I am not one to do anything slowly. Don't believe me? Ask me to go on a casual stroll through the park, and we will be speed walking the streets. Give me a project with a hard deadline, and I will have it on your desk the day before you need it. The saying, "stop and smell the roses" sounds like a nice sentiment. But who has time for that?

In a world where the phrase, "There aren't enough hours in the day!" is expressed more than the number of tocks on a clock, focusing on efficiency is an increasing need. The world has gotten smarter, smaller, and more proficient with the technology we now have available. Once, the business world had a structured 8 a.m. to 5 p.m. timeframe; employees are now able to access their work twenty-four hours a day. Staying late on a workday used to gauge the level of a successful and motivated employee. Now, it's the late-night emails and the early-morning reports that are the measuring factor of success.

The end of a workday is no longer a dividing line once the clock hits 5 p.m. or the moment you walk out of your office door. Work-life balance has been a trending term and hot topic in recent years. Having access to my emails at all hours of the day has provoked me to work without even realizing it. The ding of an email, similar to that of a text message, consumes my attention and then demands my response. So, when is it time to shut down and turn off?

If I know I am not expecting anything pressing, I will now turn my work emails off. If someone needs me, this person has my number and can (and will) call me. While working what feels like twenty-four hours a day may make you feel productive and accomplished, it also takes away from the actual quality of your work, not to mention the quality of your personal life. I know I have a different mindset at home on my couch at 8:30 p.m. than I typically have at 9 a.m. in my office. So, why respond to something that needs full attention when you are only able to give half?

> "IN A WORLD WHERE THE PHRASE,
> 'THERE AREN'T ENOUGH HOURS IN THE DAY!'
> IS EXPRESSED MORE THAN THE NUMBER OF
> TOCKS ON A CLOCK, FOCUSING ON EFFICIENCY
> IS AN INCREASING NEED."

Work-life balance is a complex issue. And in my life, the line blurs regularly. I love work and see it as my life. Sometimes it is hard to decipher when I am doing my job versus when I am living my personal life. As stated, I have been known to be out on a Saturday and start a conversation with a stranger. Next thing I know, we are exchanging business cards with plans to meet the following week to develop a potential partnership. And then there are times when I am out with a key prospect and we begin talking about Tory Burch shoes, wine, and where did that cute little clutch come from? With all of the volunteer organizations, charity galas, and the networking events, I have been lucky to find there is real truth to the phrase, "When you do something you love, you never work a day in your life."

To be honest (and consistent with the chapter), even getting to the point of doing something you love takes time. I did not always love the work I was doing, and sometimes, I still don't love the work I do. But when working hard to be successful and accomplish goals, time is a factor that must be in abundance. When I have asked different leaders about their careers, as they reflect back on their journeys, most attribute a lot of their success to the time they spent learning, studying, prospecting, or doing any other mundane task. While the other elements we discussed (opportunities, preparation, sometimes luck) are important, sometimes time is the only recourse.

I cannot tell you how many times I have been immersed in my work and looked up at the clock, thinking a minute has passed. Surprise, it's been five ... hours. As I am sure it is with most people, filling my days is not a hard feat to accomplish. Most weeks begin to look less like a calendar and more like a jigsaw puzzle, strategically fitting in meetings and coffee. Filling your day is great. But filling your day with action-oriented productivity is better.

When I was new to the Charlotte scene, I reached out to every organization I could find. Being new to an area is intimidating. But adding in the fact I needed to generate business while not knowing a single soul made the task simply daunting. People began to take me up on my requests to help volunteer for their organizations. I was asked to sit on planning committees and participate in event set-up. Who was going to turn down a volunteer?

Before I agreed to anything, I researched the opportunity entirely. I would always ask myself these specific questions:

1. WAS I PASSIONATE ABOUT THIS ORGANIZATION?
2. WOULD THIS INITIATIVE HELP BUSINESS?
3. DID I HAVE THE TIME TO FULLY COMMIT TO THE CAUSE?

I learned that questions 1 and 2 were a trade off at times and that was okay. The answer to question 3, however, had to be a resounding YES. And I had to answer at least one other question in the affirmative.

After about two months in Charlotte, one of my key prospects suggested I become involved with another nonprofit, Classroom Central. This organization raises money to provide school supplies for more than 200,000 children living in poverty in the Charlotte area. I was asked to sit in on the planning committee for the upcoming event, Brighter Better Future. Three weeks later, preparation met opportunity as a committee lead resigned, and I was asked to sit as co-chair for the event.

Co-chairing Classroom Central's event was an amazing experience. I was able to meet a lot of business leaders and incredibly talented professionals rather quickly. The time invested in this initiative was dominating. The cause was arguably not directly related to my work, so I ended up spending a lot of my own personal time working on the event. However, because I saw true benefits—both personal and professional—investing my time and energy was something I enjoyed.

At the Brighter Better Future event, I realized quickly how Charlotte had fallen victim to the "six degrees of separation" theory. I was reintroduced to multiple people who I had already briefly met at previous events, which resulted in deeper conversations and thus more solidified relationships. This was a pivotal moment for my Charlotte relocation. For the first time in a brand new area, I had been recognized. I was beginning to make a name for myself and for the company I represented.

Overall, my co-chair responsibility was a success. I wish I could say that for every initiative in which I have invested my time. Through years of experience, I have learned how to vet my ventures. While this affair was undeniably worthwhile, I have had too many more experiences that were not.

In St. Louis, I was asked to participate as a judge for a start-up community contest. I was going to be sitting alongside other leaders and guiding individuals through business plans, helping to direct their success. The focus fit within my company's area of expertise; I was passionate about entrepreneurs (in fact, I wanted to be one), and the time commitment was extremely manageable. It was a triple threat to which I said, "Count me right in!"

Fast-forward to a year later. I had received multiple emails. I had put in about forty hours of work reviewing business plans. I had not personally met a single professional. I had not been invited to attend any events. The (lacking) application process had made it seem like I would receive some true benefits for my time and efforts. However, I was so desperate to be involved and relevant in the community, I had not done my complete research on the organization or on the commitment. It was not a bad initiative by any means. It was just not what I personally needed when investing my time. And so, it was a great learning experience (because don't you love those?).

⌒ℰ⌒

I am one of those people who "always needs a project." Call it a lack of an attention span or my overactive mind, but I always find myself seeking out my next project in which to invest my time. After wrapping up my role with Classroom Central, I found I had a plethora of free time. While my co-chair role had given me a name for a fleeting second in the Charlotte skyline, I knew it was not enough to have people lining up at my front door, begging me to participate in their next initiative. If I wanted a new cause on which to focus, I would have to find it. And so, I did.

I mentioned in an earlier chapter my involvement with the United Way of the Central Carolinas. As stated, I met Tina, one of the Senior VPs at the company, and quickly became thankful for her energy, passion, and objectives. Tina was hired on to lead the United Way of the Central Carolinas toward a new initiative of engaging the community and involving leaders. At our first meeting, I was incredibly impressed with her passion for getting women involved in the organization, and she was thrilled to learn about my experience in leading a 3,500-plus-member women's leadership society. This is when I discovered my next initiative upon which to focus: I wanted to work with Tina to start a Central Carolinas' Women's Leadership Council.

As I sit here writing, this initiative is currently underway. I am hopeful that through this initiative, my colleagues and I can create a more successful and beneficial society. I am hopeful that by the time you read this book, I will have more to report on with the women's council in Charlotte. But if not, and if the idea never gets off the ground, at least I can add it to my ever-growing list of lessons learned. Because like they say, fall down seven times, get up eight. Or like it is in real life, fall down ninety-seven times, get up ninety-eight.

Success takes time. And as we have already confirmed, we need more of it. So, when you are racing the clock and being ruled by a calendar, the people, organizations, and events with which you fill your day need to be of value. This will be—and should be—a uniquely different process to everyone. Even some meetings that will provide great value to you will be nothing more than a favor and a free cup of coffee to the other person. Be aware of that difference and be grateful for others' time just as you would like someone to be of your time.

While working in business development, the CEO came to me with a new requirement: set up ten meetings each week, or two meetings per day. Sounds obtainable. Sure, it is manageable to find, invite, secure, and confirm two meetings each day or ten meetings each week, forty meetings each month, and nearly five hundred meetings each year. (And all of those meetings require proper vetting beforehand as well as professional follow up.) But why? Of course, there is power in numbers. But there is more power in *value*.

One of the most important things I learned in networking and time management is when and why to set meetings. While it is great to always network and follow up with a conversation, be aware of the time involved. I've been one to set meetings simply for the sake of setting meetings. However, walking away without a call to action is really just a waste of time and energy. I used to take every meeting that was requested of me. I was guilty of requesting meetings to fulfill this ten-meetings-per-week quota. What I learned, though, is that it only wasted time—mine, the company's, the other individual's, and even the barista's! I now only ask to set meetings when I have a request, reason, or purpose behind them.

Networking is fabulous, and I will always follow up with an email. But I learned true follow-up does not always require a get-together. And not only is that okay, it is appreciated. Still, always keep your contacts in hand and stay in touch as previously discussed. More than likely, there may come a time where there is a call to action and you will be glad to have had that interaction to be able to circle back to. As stated earlier, it's all about timing.

❦

Does anyone else hate when someone asks, "Where do you find the time?" I always respond with the same statement. I say, "I don't find time. I make time to save time." Okay, hear me out.

Everything takes time. I have gotten to the point where prioritizing mine (and monetizing it) has come to save me (and my sanity). Look for ways to combine two things to create more time. Working out and work: take your conference calls on your AirPods while on a walk in the park. Go for long runs in corporate parks, in search of new businesses to prospect. Also, look for time-demanding activities you can either a.) cut out, b.) simplify, or c.) outsource.

In a world where there is quite literally an app and device for everything, take advantage of technology. I bought a robot vacuum so I could cut out vacuuming. I read *The Skimm* daily so I can simplify how I consume the daily news. And I outsource my cleaning—because it takes me six hours to clean my tiny apartment and the $70/month is worth getting that time back to relax, catch up, hang out, and *live*. Okay. You're up. Where are you making time?

We need to stop pretending work-life balance is an easily defined notion or that it is always obtainable. I visualize my work and my personal life as two entirely separate things on either side of a seesaw. (Side note: are seesaws still a thing?) Sometimes my work demands my full attention and my personal life takes a dive. I have less time to call my family, I miss wine nights with my girlfriends, and I skip workouts. And then there are other times when someone in my family or a friend needs my entire focus. My family still lives in the Midwest, so if something is going on, large or small, sometimes I just need to drop what I'm doing, jump on a flight, and head home.

While looking at your personal life and professional life as a seesaw, imagine yourself in the middle, the single pivot point that enables the board to teeter back and forth. If this pivot point is broken, damaged, or otherwise not working, neither side will function. Meaning, if you are tired, stressed, worn down, etc., you cannot give your best effort to either side. And then no one wins.

Take care of yourself. Take personal time and enjoy it, guilt-free.

About ten years ago, I started a little tradition I call "Having a Betsy Day," with the focus of "my day, my way." I take the day off from work, turn off my phone, and create an agenda full of carefree activities I enjoy, like getting up early for a walk with coffee, reading a book start to finish, going for a long run, going to lunch alone at a local favorite spot, and lying out in the sun somewhere just thinking. These days are incredible. And incredibly rejuvenating!

There is a time for everything. A time to invest in yourself and a time to reflect. A time to take a [insert your name here] Day and a time to bury yourself in work. A time to network and a time to follow up. A time to work hard and a time to play. Time flies and life is demanding. Regardless of what you decide to fill your time with, make sure it makes you feel complete and full.

As my career continues, I don't always have the ability to enjoy a full Betsy Day. However, I will take smaller-scale moments in which to indulge. For example, I love getting my quick mani-pedi, one hour of true relaxation and bliss when I physically am not able to touch my phone, enabling me to get lost in my thoughts. On days when I can get away, I let my boss and team know about my temporary unavailability, and out I go, no guilt allowed. I encourage you to do the same. Whether you take a break to get your nails done, get a blowout, take a yoga class, or FaceTime with a cute nephew (or is that just mine?), do what you enjoy. Sometimes you are able to break away for an hour and other times only five minutes. So, throw a little umbrella in your coffee and soak in the moment. Take the time—but most importantly, *make* the time.

CHAPTER 9

Our Obligation to the Community

I am going to let you in on a little secret. I am extremely passionate about the community in which I live. Okay, right. So. That better not have been too big of a revelation.

Growing up in a middle class, comfortable family, I can remember my family participating in community events and fundraisers. At the time, I had no idea what that meant, other than the fact that whoever got to put the envelope in the church basket was clearly the favorite child that week, or that spaghetti dinners held in our elementary gymnasium meant being able to run and hide under the bleachers. Does anyone else miss that old game where you essentially walk in a circle and land on different numbers while music plays, and when the music stops, the person standing on the given number wins a cake? Let's. Bring. This. Back!

I have had the opportunity to attend the YWCA Metro St. Louis Women of Distinction awards luncheon for five consecutive years. Each year, they highlight high-powered women who have created a lasting impact in business and the community. And each year, while I enjoy celebrating all of these women, the one category that always intrigues me the most is that of "Future Leader."

The "Future Leader" designation typically goes to a young woman in grade school who has dedicated herself to the community. Each of these young women has truly inspired me. These girls—literally children—have done more for their communities in their ten years of life than some I know in the ten years since graduating high school! They have created reading programs for their peers, worked to solve cyber-bullying, and taken active and admired steps to end hunger for our homeless. While I grew up in an environment that promoted giving back and community engagement, unfortunately, that was not where my energy was focused.

༄

At Alleman, my Catholic high school, we were required to complete one hundred hours of community service to graduate. An incredible opportunity to learn the importance of giving back was, in my case, unfortunately exchanged for the ability to identify the best way to get out of a project. I wish I had taken advantage of this assignment—or at the bare minimum, taken it seriously. It is not that I did not care about the community; it was simply not where my priorities lay at that time .

My university, Illinois State (go you Redbirds, go!), also promoted community investment. College was the place where I first heard the term "philanthropy" and where I realized its importance. After I joined the sorority Gamma Phi Beta (love in ΠKE!), I quickly learned about the sorority's charitable mission. Gamma Phi Beta strives to provide experiences and resources that build spiritual, mental, and social resiliency in girls. My chapter (Delta Pi) focused on an organization in which to raise funds in order to support their mission. While the efforts here were not extensive, they were focused on community and what it means to give (financially) and to give back (volunteering). This was my first interaction with fundraising. Foreshadowing?

While in college, I began working for a local minor league hockey team, the Bloomington PrairieThunder (which no longer exists, RIP). I was working in the Community Relations department and was able to participate in multiple initiatives. In an outwardly-facing position, I began to identify what a true community relations-, development-, events-focused position looked like, and I realized I loved it.

Energizing the community in turn energized me. I learned about all of the factors and details that went into various local programs and initiatives. I learned I loved being a part of something bigger than me. Due to lease difficulties, management change, and mergers, the team ceased to exist (pour one out for the PrairieThunder). However, the experience sparked a fire in me to find a similar professional experience. Thus, I found my way to and began working for United Way.

Throughout my previous mentions about United Way, I hope it is clear that it was a position filled with true purpose and passion. The role with this amazing organization continued to develop my desire to engage in the community. And when I left United Way, I was extremely fortunate to be invited to sit on their Women's Leadership Society Cabinet as a member and event chair.

Throughout my time at United Way, as well as after, I have both been asked and have requested to sit on various boards. Collectively, I have been directly involved with more than ten organizations within the past three years. Participating in these initiatives is a true obligation that requires time, energy, and money. However, as current and future leaders, we need to see the importance in these responsibilities and see them as not only opportunities, but our civic duties as well.

Civic social responsibility is the desire for a corporation to participate in the community in a form of "giving back" and "doing good." Companies see the need to support organizations that align with their corporate or personal missions, financially and in the form of volunteer hours. Their participation usually lies outside of business requirements.

> "THERE IS ALWAYS A NEED IN OUR WORLD, NATION, AND COMMUNITY TO HELP OUT. AS CITIZENS, WE NEED TO IDENTIFY THESE NEEDS. AND AS LEADERS, WE NEED TO PROMOTE AND SUPPORT THEM."

Working for both a nonprofit and for a corporate company in St. Louis, I was able to see firsthand the importance of philanthropy and our civic social responsibility. It was not until I moved away that I realized how fortunate I had been to work in St. Louis, where I was able to see the true generosity of so many large corporations. Witnessing multiple Fortune 500 companies dedicate their missions to the organizations and initiatives in need reaffirmed the importance of my own civic, social responsibility.

I need to be involved. And my involvement needs to mean something and provide an impact. While my board seat experience indisputably catapulted my career and expanded my professional network, I was able to fulfill a role. I was able to successfully help with a cause, raise money for underprivileged children, find a cure for multiple sclerosis, secure a safe haven for battered women, enable food kitchens to operate, and much more.

⁓

There is always a need in our world, nation, and community to help out. As citizens, we need to identify these needs. And as leaders, we need to promote and support them. It is easy to get lost in the sea of "will-you-donate-to-my-cause" solicitations. It's not hard to get caught up in the moment after a terrible natural disaster, quickly donating $1 to the victims in the latest tsunami. However, it's the lack of education that hurts, rather than promotes, the causes.

Let's look back at the 2014 ALS Ice Bucket Challenge. The ALS (amyotrophic lateral sclerosis, or Lou Gehrig's disease) Ice Bucket Challenge was a true phenomenon in which people poured a bucket of ice water over their heads, donated money to the organization, and nominated friends and family to participate. The challenge quickly went viral with more than one million people participating, raising more than $115 million.

The ALS Ice Bucket Challenge was incredibly successful in raising both money and awareness for the disease. While I am sure the 2014 donor base was a peak year for ALS, I believe there are some concrete lessons on which we can capitalize from this example. The challenge got people excited and encouraged them to join a nationwide phenomenon through utilizing individual social media platforms. The organization was able to provide a stage to enable learning and make the giving process easy and fun, while using people's relationships as a catalyst to reach out to more people. Most nonprofits can only dream about reaching this level of connection and outreach.

While this was an extraordinary event, the *uniqueness* of the campaign made it successful. Repeating the event will most likely not repeat its results. So then, how exactly can we help nonprofits achieve success?

⟐

I believe current and future business leaders have the responsibility to help organizations with their missions. Large corporations will host a corporate giving campaign, enabling but not always encouraging employees to donate to a cause. Some companies conduct a campaign with limited options for giving, whereas others allow employees to choose from an endless list of organizations and causes to support. Despite these efforts, I have learned a lot of people have the "someone else will take care of it" mindset. I want to ask these people: like who? The someone else sitting next to you, also thinking someone else will get involved?

Large companies have been truly fundamental in terms of community support. Some companies will align themselves to a few organizations and see to it that their budgets are planned to include sizable donations.

Bank of America is known for being a leader because of its charitable generosity. Within every community where I have lived (St. Louis, Dallas, and Charlotte), Bank of America has also been a leader in civic social responsibility. The company is currently a trailblazer in community investment; according to its website, Bank of America has given and continues to give more than $2 billion to address immediate concerns as well as innovative solutions for economic needs over the past ten years. Through its support, Bank of America promotes long-term economic growth and improved quality of life. [1]

Many other companies—large, midsize, and small—have similar focuses. The support of nonprofits and various community initiatives through financial means is often present in objectives and mission statements. Event sponsorship dollars and corporate gifts play large roles in charity fundraising. However, as important as these large contributions may be, fundraising should not simply end there. Individuals need to also step up to the table.

Corporations have been moving away from enforcing their employees to take part in civic social responsibility. I have been told that, in previous generations, people would walk into their new jobs with multiple forms to sign and one of those was a pledge card for any given nonprofit they wanted to support. The mindset was that as employees of a given company, it was not where you gave but that you gave. Now, it is rare employees get asked to donate at all during the entirety of their tenures.

When you have bills, needs, wants, it is hard to justify giving money to some unknown charity in some unknown place. So, educate yourself. Discover what issues are important to you. Learn about initiatives and causes happening in your area and how even a small monthly gift can save lives. When I talk to various people about the organizations in which they participate, I rarely see passion and excitement with their response. And yet there are so many causes and organizations out there to feel passionate and excited about! Sometimes I ask if a person's company runs a United Way campaign (I suppose I'm a creature of habit). It kills me when the response is either 1. I don't know. 2. Yes, but I don't give. Or, the worst of all, 3. What's that?

As a young professional, I have been invited to numerous young professional events. These events range from cocktails to galas to happy hours. Despite the differences these events may have, the one constant variable is the solicitation of a monetary gift.

It actually offends me when people attend such nonprofit events and become outraged when they are asked for money. When I attend a charitable event, no matter what the cause, I keep in mind that the primary goal of the event is to raise money.

---

1 "Making an impact: Driving economic & social progress," Bank of America, accessed July 1, 2018, https://about.bankofamerica.com/en-us/what-guides-us/driving-social-and-economic-progress.html#f-bid=tzDZNQa1pXJ.

I attended a local event for a relatively large and well-known not-for-profit organization in Charlotte. It was promoted as a young professionals' cocktail event. This was my first event in this new metro, and I was excited. I left for the event in my favorite LBD (little black dress), heels, and with my credit card ready to be run.

I walked into the room and immediately thought I was in the wrong place. There was a great crowd of people, but most of them were in jeans. Not off to the best start. I proceeded with caution and tried to gauge the fellow attendees. I overheard some conversation that the unlimited drinks only included beer and wine. *Okay, fair argument,* I thought. For a $100 ticket, liquor is usually included, though in my experience, liquor does make anyone's purse strings looser. After an hour, I quickly reassessed my stance on the liquor issue. The number one priority at this event was drinking. I asked one of the staff members if there were going to be a presentation of some kind or an opportunity to give. She looked confused.

I left the young professionals' event embarrassed. The crowd seemed to feel their presence at the event proved their prerogative to receive free cocktails and food. I was confused at how the event was funded. What was the point of actually hosting the event? Mostly, I was disappointed in the organization for allowing such an ineffective and counterproductive event to be organized.

As a Millennial, I believe we need to step up in the business world and the community. Participating in an organization is not slapping a sticker on your newest social media profile and drinking at the next cocktail event. Millennials need to give back in both time and treasure and see it as their responsibility as up-and-coming leaders.

Millennials cannot give at the same rate as Baby Boomers who are retiring. That is an undeniable fact. But Baby Boomers did not start at the level they are currently at today. They began to donate, cultivated relationships, and their gifts grew. Millennials, we should be groomed now for giving. We should put donating into our budgets and increase our gifts as our salaries rise.

To Baby Boomers and Gen X-ers: we need you to invite us Millennials (plus iGens, Gen Alphas, and so on) into the room, into the events, into the conversations that enable us to learn and want to engage and then give. It is an interesting time with the concept of fundraising evolving. As a Millennial, I want to see/need to have more transparency for where my money is going. I want to be a part of the process and see concrete results. As giving needs change, let's change how we ask for money, as well.

I have been to more galas than I can count, meaning I have more ballgowns than closet space. While the experience of these gala nights and the wow factor of the photo booths and fancy cocktails may have worn off for me, it is not lost on me that there is a strong need to include others. I have invited numerous friends to their first galas, and I take pride in that fact. I have walked into far too many ballrooms as the youngest person in attendance. Do we need to encourage and invite Millennials to attend such events, or do we need to look at what Millennials are willing to attend and give to?

Fundraising is a multifaceted and complex topic and one that is at the very core of the foundation upon which my career was built. Fundraising is clearly evolving, but as with anything that evolves, there are questions, concerns, and a lack of clarity on what exactly is to come next.

Our community is built on the support of the corporations, organizations, and people within it. It is well-known that the number one reason why people don't give is because they are not asked to give. So, I am standing here, asking you to give. I don't care about what you support, but I urge you to find your philanthropic passion and create your purpose. As leaders, advocates, and activists, we need to see civic social responsibility as an obligation.

So, will *you* give?

CHAPTER 10

Challenge Accepted

Wouldn't it be just fabulous if our careers consisted of running through fields of wildflowers while twirling and laughing, getting more new opportunities than we could ever dream of, and being promoted every other year? Then, we would simply retire our successful hats on the million-dollar shelves and dive into our pools of rubies or fly off into the sunset in our Airbus A380 private jets. Yes, that would be just fabulous.

But, ultimately, would it mean anything?

Life is full of challenges. This statement is a fact, one you can always count on. And the best (or maybe the worst) part is that challenges don't come in a one-size-fits-all option; instead, they pop up at the most inopportune and random of times and are never as you expected. In times when you cannot control the outcome of a situation, the best thing to do is focus on the *way* you handle it.

The way you deal with a challenge speaks volumes about your character. "What was your biggest challenge and how did you deal with it?" Who hasn't heard this question in an interview or during an interview briefing? Why is this question so popular and prevalent? It is because challenges occur and there really is no way around them, only through them.

Through many experiences, I've learned that challenges provide a catalyst for growth. I have seen my dad, who lives with multiple sclerosis, work through some of the most difficult challenges an individual is forced to face. After witnessing my dad overcome so much, there has never been a time where I have come through a challenge without learning something. Whether my approach was off, or I miscalculated the input needed, I have gained essential knowledge I clearly did not have before.

Looking back over my career and even before that to my days in sports, I realize there has been a consistent theme: I surround myself with challenges. I thrive from overcoming obstacles. I love putting myself in situations where I need to work my way up.

I grew up competing in gymnastics at an elite level. This sport forces athletes to challenge themselves regularly. All basic, compulsory skills are used to flip faster, higher, longer. Gymnastics is a sport that challenges not only the body, but also the mind. Fall one time on that five foot tall, four-inch wide balance beam and try to say you're not scared or at least nervous about getting back up there seconds later to repeat the same skill. In gymnastics, you have no choice. Pounding out routine after routine on the uneven bars with blisters the size of quarters is a daily occurrence. From this sport, I was able to learn how to push through hardships and challenges.

While I loved gymnastics, the practices were not always enjoyable. I remember feeling an overwhelming sense of anxiety driving to the gym, knowing I had to work on a new skill that terrified me. I remember long summer days when our strength conditioning rotation lasted an extra hour and it was followed by another hour of flexibility training. There were times when I would leave the gym bruised, sore, sweaty, and feeling defeated. Still, I loved the sport. And the thrill of landing a perfect routine was energizing and made every ounce of hardship worth it.

Gymnastics was a sport where poise was necessary and confidence was transparent. Wearing a leotard, performing in front of hundreds of people, with four judges critiquing my every move, I gained my strong sense of self-esteem. Competitions were hard, but at the end of the meet, there was no one I could blame for my performance other than myself. Whether it was a fear of an apparatus or the difficulty in learning a new skill, I was forced to work through my challenges on my own.

Gymnastics shaped my work ethic. I face challenges in the workforce similarly to those in the gym. I don't give up and go home because I am unable to complete a task, unsure how to proceed with a report, unsuccessful in contacting someone. I focus on the end result of what I am doing, and while hardships arise, getting through them and landing in success makes my effort worth it.

While at United Way, working with the Women's Leadership Society, I would strive to put myself in the room of senior leaders where I was of the lowest level. I truly believe if you are always the smartest person in the room, you are in the wrong room. I loved to sit in the boardroom and absorb the wealth of knowledge that was present. Participating in these high-level conversations enabled me to learn firsthand

and forced me to stay current on all topics business. Through these interactions, I made an astounding realization: some things are not taught in school, cannot be read about in books, are not displayed in newspapers, and are not spoken about in the office. Sometimes, simply observing a roundtable of leaders or contributing to a discussion provides immense intellectual insights.

> "WHILE LEARNING FROM OTHERS AND GROWING TOGETHER MAY NOT ALWAYS BE A REALISTIC OUTCOME, IT WILL ALWAYS BE THE RESPECTABLE ONE. LEARN HOW YOU INTERACT WITH OTHERS AND, MORE IMPORTANTLY, LEARN HOW OTHERS PERCEIVE YOU."

Sitting in a boardroom, I observed these business leaders converse and connect and form relationships, which lead to direct business transactions. I overheard leaders discussing promising young professionals to watch. I witnessed business associates commit to high-value donations. All I absorbed truly inspired me. And ever since then, I have challenged myself to regularly be in contact with people who are smarter than I am. I like to place myself in situations where it is impossible not just to learn, but to grow as well.

I have for a long time practiced the method of placing myself in challenging situations or surrounding myself with people who challenge me. But when unforeseen challenges appear, they can cause mayhem and chaos.

I am sure everyone has dealt with that one team member who is an ultimate pain. While I hope no one is reading this thinking, "Yep, and her name is Betsy," I would be remiss to think I have earned a gold star on every team in which I have participated. Not all personalities mesh, and not all people work well together. See these situations as additional opportunities for your own personal and professional growth.

Whether you work on a team is sometimes out of your control. But keep your focus on the big picture, the project at hand. Having Baby Boomers, Gen X-ers, and Millenials all in the workplace together is the perfect recipe for turmoil. Different upbringings and backgrounds are sure to produce different insights, techniques, and methodologies. And while learning from others and growing together may not always be a realistic outcome, it will always be the respectable one. Learn how you interact with others and, more importantly, learn how others perceive you.

One of my largest challenges was learning about and understanding my own interpersonal skills. Working with a new colleague, I was unable to have much face-to-face time with him as I worked out of a different office. Our main source of communication became emails. As anyone who has had a conversation with me will agree, I am animated, bubbly, and passionate (which is a much nicer word for "loud"). However, when I communicate via text, my messages tend to be direct. While I may speak in all caps and my sentences might end with seven or eight exclamation points, in emails and text messages, I will be straightforward, answering more curtly with a "Yes. Thanks so much" response. My colleague, who had witnessed my personality in person and sat in on conference call discussions, was taken aback with my seemingly short responses.

I learned responses in the form of texts leave a lot of room for uncertainty. Communicating through text messaging eliminates the use of tone, which drives the emotion behind the discussion. I was surprised to find out my new colleague thought I was rude and unfriendly. While it is not something I am proud of, it taught me how to soften my responses and how picking up the phone, while a bit more time-consuming, is a lot more personable. If only all challenges were this easy to resolve.

The workplace offers all types of challenges—from trying to close a deal to technical constraints to employee disagreements, all the way to not having Coca-Cola products in the vending machine (the worst). Despite any obstacle that may arise, it is important to remember challenges are not there to knock you over and keep you down, but rather to push you back up so you can find a new way forward.

⟅⟆

What is my largest challenge? My age. I will be the first to admit I am young but look younger (I know, I know. "You'll be thankful for this someday," friends tell me). During those high-level meetings in important boardrooms, how am I supposed to ensure I have clout and true business insight when some people see me as nothing more than a child who snuck her way into the room?

One time I was meeting with a business leader. We were having a great conversation at a well-populated Starbucks. Two of the leader's colleagues walked in and approached our table excitedly. "Is this your daughter?" they asked. The person's daughter was nineteen years old. About a decade off. Seemed like a harmless and innocent mistake, but multiply this scenario by almost every encounter I have.

I learned to take this kind of interaction in stride. (I am still learning how to take it as a compliment as so many people tell me to do.) However, I have approached the subject in a new way. When I am meeting with an established business leader, I will acknowledge my age. Without disclosing the number (a girl never tells, right?), I will put the issue of my youth on the table. I will acknowledge that while I may be young, I do not lack experience or insight. I will divulge some of my top opportunities and discuss my track record for success. I might not be able to change someone's opinion, but no one can argue with fact. Someone can very well think I am young and inexperienced (their opinion). But no one can argue against my success in raising more than $13 million in one year for United Way or that I obtained five new clients within five months in a new market and competitive city (fact and fact).

Own your successes because they are yours; you have earned them. You are in the room for a reason. It is easy to look around the table and compare yourself to others, but here is the thing—you will never win this little game. Isn't it scary that, by comparison, "good" can oh so easily become "not good enough"? Well, I am here (in the most sincere, non-cliché way) to tell you that you are indeed good *and* good enough. You earned your spot at that table, so sit in your chair and lean back (just kidding, lean in), proving to them why you are there.

Society views age as a direct ratio to success. The older the age, the more knowledge someone holds. While my age is a factor I cannot change, the connotation behind it is something I *can* change. When speaking with C-level leaders, an age difference is very much noticeable. However, I refuse to let that difference speak for my competency or my abilities. I do everything in my power to enable people to see me as more than a number.

The most interesting thing about challenges is they force us to look at the same issues in new ways. Challenges keep life exciting. How boring success would be if the road to victory were flat and easy. What would you celebrate and cheers your champagne to? I always get the best rush of accomplishment after overcoming my largest challenges. While I cannot imagine sitting, working diligently on a project, all the while just hoping for a huge challenge to come crashing in like a tsunami, I do believe challenges are a necessary part of success and I am thankful for them. (Though usually much, much after the fact). Without them, it would not be a worthwhile journey.

My move to Charlotte was a tremendous opportunity, though it was simultaneously a massive challenge. I had no contacts in North Carolina. The company had no clients in the metropolitan area. All I had was my makeshift CRM (client relationship management) document, the *Business Journal's* Book of Lists, and my strategy. While I had a track record of success on my side, I was embarking on a journey that was saturated with challenges.

From filling my day with meetings, to having a day too full of meetings; from being directionally challenged (why do the roads in Charlotte change names every other block?), to being unprepared for side road traffic; I encountered multiple challenges daily. With each challenge that was thrown at me, I would focus intently, doing my best to work through it. Some challenges were easy and I learned a lot from them. Others were ridiculous and felt as though their only purpose was just to provide stress.

One of the biggest and best lessons I learned through this series of challenges was how to overcome rejection and the fear of the unknown. I picked up my entire life, stepped outside of my comfort zone (734 miles outside, to be exact), and took a leap of faith. I was forced to learn that rejection was unavoidable and unrelenting. Rejection in the form of declined meetings and unanswered calls was tolerable. What became intolerable and demoralizing was learning I often got pity meetings. Yes, it had come to the point where I had reached out so many times, people felt sorry for me and accepted my invitation to meet—not to truly talk, but to get me to (ever-so-kindly) stop reaching out. How do I know those meetings were pity meetings? Oh, the people I met with ended up letting me know outright in words more colorful than a box of crayons. So, there it was. I had to overcome this challenge and many other forms of rejection with the ability to reenergize and refocus.

The fear of the unknown is a challenge that sometimes has no other remedy except for having faith and dedication. Through my unwavering commitment to success, I was able to take comfort in the unknown because I was doing everything in my power to encourage success. And while I don't think I will ever be completely "in the know," taking such a large leap into the infinite abyss before me taught me how to proceed in times of uncertainty. Unfortunately, most challenges don't come with warnings or aftermath statuses (but oh, how I so wish they did!).

All together, these challenges built character and provided me a platform to stand upon. After obtaining my first three clients, I was able to wear my accomplishments like a badge of honor. And even though I was far from succeeding in my larger goals at that stage, the little triumphs were the stepping-stones that lead me to succeed in climbing my figurative professional mountain.

ᏀᏅ

Now, is anyone else still unnerved by the "Us pretty girls have to accept that" comment my former mentor made regarding success? It was a true challenge I did not know what to do with. Yes, I am young woman. But does that mean I need to allow my accomplishments to be aligned with how others view my appearance and whether they consider me a "pretty girl"?

In a time when women are so intensely focused on defining ourselves as equals and stepping up to the podium to share our much-needed voices, how dare anybody even utter the words "pretty girl"?

I worked so hard to create my success based on my work ethic and track record. One evening, I was presented with an inappropriate offer from a high-powered business prospect. Young and slightly unnerved, I approached my boss to discuss this experience with her, and her response sent physical shockwaves through my body. She said, "What are you doing to allow this man to approach you? We need to keep him as a partner."

Blame.

What was *I* doing? My subsequent self-reflection lead me to confusion, guilt, and shame. ... Until those feelings turned into anger. What was *I* doing to allow this man to approach me? I was doing nothing. I was building a business relationship and working for the company. I showed up, worked hard, and trusted you, the CEO, as my boss, as a leader, as a woman. I did not give this man permission to approach me in a non-professional manner. And by working for you, I needed (and expected) you to trust me. To support me, help me, guide me, advocate for me—not accuse me. And most certainly, not to take his side.

In a world where women are trying to equalize ourselves, we cannot allow this type of blame to occur. We need to support each other, not victimize our peers, employees, and colleagues. It is disheartening enough when men objectify women, but when *women* objectify women, it is demoralizing. And ladies, we are better than that.

Success is a staircase. Climb one stair at a time and celebrate the little victory before moving up to the next one. No victory is too little to celebrate and no obstacle is too big to overcome. Trust me, I literally cheers my champagne to a week of no rejected emails. Because sometimes, you need to celebrate the small things.

As I continue on my career path in hopes of leaping toward success, I know many more challenges will come my way. Some will be small, providing little lessons as I work through them, and others will be hurricanes that may blow me off course completely before I hopefully find my way again. Regardless, I will keep my head held high and try to overcome each obstacle with grace, poise, and a new lesson learned. I am determined to succeed and prepared to conquer whatever comes my way. So life, if you want to throw me a curve ball ...

... challenge accepted.

CHAPTER 11

You Failed

You failed.

Famous last words.

Or are they?

My mom loves telling this story about when I was two years old. I walked up to her and asked for a cookie. She said, "Sure, you can have a cookie." I looked at her and smiled, now asking, "Can I have two cookies?" "Okay," my mom agreed, "you can have two cookies." I instantly hit her back with, "Can I have three cookies?" My mom stared at me. She decided to see how far I was going to really go with this. Seven. I asked for *seven* cookies until she finally said, "No! You can have one cookie!"

Clearly, I failed in whatever I was trying to accomplish there. But at least I went for what I wanted.

On the road to success, challenges are the expected and yet unexpected roadblocks and detours. They are a catalyst for reevaluating, redirecting, and continuing on. However, on the winding road of your career, what happens when you come to a complete and absolute dead end, exhausting all of your resources? That is known as "failure." And while failure is the end of the road, it is not the end of the journey.

Most think the opposite of success is failure. However, while failure is undoubtedly the absence of success, it is not absolute. And while we can all agree that failing is less than ideal, failing needs to be seen as not the end of, but a part of, the journey.

⟨⟩

The other night, I was watching a 2005 rom-com movie, *Elizabethtown*. While I was randomly watching this movie thanks to Netflix's personalized "chosen for you" suggestions, I found myself pleasantly shocked at some of the messages behind the film.

The movie tells the story of Drew Baylor (Orlando Bloom), a shoe designer at an athletic apparel conglomerate. After eight years developing the shoe that is supposed to revolutionize the industry, Drew's product results in a catastrophic failure, costing the company $1 billion, resulting in the loss of his career. As he is about to carry out his plan to take his own life, Drew receives news of his father's death. Drew returns to his dad's Kentucky hometown, Elizabethtown, to bring home his body. On the flight there, Drew meets the lovely Claire (Kirsten Dunst), a lighthearted flight attendant who tries to help him face his fiasco and embrace life.

Watching Drew deal with his failure was indicative of the pitfalls that follow a blow to success. And for anyone who has experienced failure (which is hopefully everyone), it was a reminder failure is not the end of the journey.

In one scene, Claire confronts Drew about his catastrophe. The dialogue captures the essence of failure so brilliantly, I replayed it almost five times (okay, fine, twelve). At the end of a long monologue about failure, Claire says, "Have the courage to fail big and stick around."

Just sit back and let those words sink in. "Fail big and stick around." So. Much. Yes. I cannot help but love everything about this proclamation. Failure defeats you in every sense of the word. It knocks you off your pedestal and onto your knees, suffocates your energy, and cripples your next move. But Claire depicts the aftermath impeccably. Allow yourself to wallow (an appropriate amount), and then move on and continue your journey. True greatness is not success without failure; it is success despite failure. And no matter how minuscule or vast the failure may seem, feel, or be, do not give up.

> "ALLOW YOURSELF TO WALLOW (AN APPROPRIATE AMOUNT), AND THEN MOVE ON AND CONTINUE YOUR JOURNEY. TRUE GREATNESS IS NOT SUCCESS WITHOUT FAILURE; IT IS SUCCESS DESPITE FAILURE; IT IS SUCCESS DESPITE FAILURE."

Earlier, I spoke about my job-seeking adventure. I sent out ninety-eight applications to ninety-eight jobs. And I failed to get ninety-seven of those jobs. Those were ninety-seven disappointments that resulted in ninety-seven setbacks. Ninety-seven true-life failures. Ninety-am-I-ever-going-to-crawl-out-of-this-depressingly-endless-cycle-of-rejection-seven. There were times when I wanted to give in and settle for some mediocre job instead of continuing my pursuit for the career I really wanted. And let me tell you how scared my parents were when I almost *did* settle for a serving position at a local bar.

I didn't succumb to my defeat. I may have changed directions, objectives, paths ... but I did not change my goal of securing a job I wanted. I kept sending out resumes, filling out applications, and reaching out to hiring managers. Each rejection letter motivated me to send out three more submissions. In an idiosyncratic way, I felt each failure brought me closer to success, which thankfully was what happened when I *finally* (emphasis on finally) did land my first job.

I learned to embrace failure in a way that reenergized my efforts and reinforced my need to succeed. "Fail fast" is a phrase I have come to know, admire, and portray. I wish I could say I never fail; however, I have started to realize that I fail every single day. And after that revelation, I learned I had two options: to dwell in the pity of it and give up, or to learn from what happened and keep going. Okay, so I really only had one option. And so do you.

Let's go back to that statement. Did you catch it? I fail. Every. Single. Day. From (not) securing meetings to creating (un)impactful events, I fail. I've sent emails without subject lines; I've forgotten meetings that were clearly on my calendar; I've even failed to provide a much-needed report to my boss by the mutually agreed upon deadline. Have you ever had a conversation and after walking away, replayed it in your mind countless times, each one with a better, smarter approach? (My hand awkwardly rises.) No one talks about failing. As a society, we have moved toward portraying the imagery of a picture-perfect, cookie-cutter life. But it simply does not exist.

Arianna Huffington is the co-founder and editor-in-chief of the Pulitzer Prize-winning *Huffington Post*, a nationally syndicated columnist, radio host, and author of fourteen books. However, when Arianna first started out in her career, thirty-six publishers rejected her. Despite these failings, Arianna succeeded. When speaking about her success, Arianna stated, "[A] key component of whatever successes I've had has been what I've learned from my failures."[2]

What intrigues me most about success is the number of times people failed before they reached their breakthrough moments. Arianna was rejected thirty-six times. Thomas Edison failed 1,000 times before creating the light bulb. Walt Disney was fired from his first job because he lacked creativity. Dr. Seuss was rejected by twenty-seven different publishers, while novelist Stephen King was rejected by thirty publishers. All of these people are now highly recognizable public figures, successful in their fields.

---

2 "9 Founders that Bounced Back from Failure to Build Successful Companies," *pressfarm*, accessed July 1, 2018, https://press.farm/founders-bounced-back-failure-build-successful-companies/.

If challenges are speed bumps that redirect you or slow you down, failing is the complete end of the road. Crash and burn, you're done? No, crash and exit vehicle, reassess, recalibrate, and reignite. These times of failure are the most important times, not only to learn, but to keep going. When most people get to the ends of their ropes, they let go, move on, and chalk it up as a loss. However, that is the time when you need to step back, evaluate what happened, understand what went wrong and then try again. While inventing the light bulb, Thomas Edison said it best: "I have not failed. I have just found 1,000 ways that it won't work."

This is all easier said than done. As I said in the prologue, it is easy for those who have already succeeded to put on their rose-colored glasses and tell their tales in the form of "how to" books, which always include times of failure depicted in the context of the story's climax. Thomas Edison's quote would be nothing more than a joke if he had never fulfilled his goal of creating the light bulb. He kept pursuing his goal and so should we. Our successes may not be as fruitful or well-known as others', but that does not make them any less important.

There were so many times in life when I felt failure. Roaming through my high school, believing I was unable to break out of the average mold, I felt like a failure. When I was rejected from the University of Illinois, where my entire family (including cousins, aunts, and uncles) went: hello, failure! I even failed two classes (accounting and calculus) in college. (I'm putting this in print, embarrassingly enough, in hope of encouraging someone else.)

Let's examine these failures. First off, is there anyone who is actually good at calculus? (Dad, put your hand down.) I was never good at math. I have nightmares of the days when I would sit at the kitchen table, far into the night, my dad trying relentlessly to explain to me why the alphabet was taking over my math book and that X in fact *did* equal Y, which was by the way a recurring factor of -7 over .25.

In college, I tried (truly, I did) so hard to succeed in calculus and accounting. I went to my professors' office hours and had my friends study with me. Every time I thought I logically understood a problem, it would be completely wrong. If I could have ripped out every single strand of my hair, I probably would have. Inside, with increasing frustration, I just kept asking, "WHY?" Why did I not understand? Why could I not comprehend these questions? Why was I not getting the correct answer? I felt completely incompetent.

In the midst of failing business classes and searching for what I was going to do next, I was drifting. Like a leaf, I was floating. I was trying on different identities to see what fit, what resonated. In this process, I learned the importance of roots. Like anchors that hold large oak trees in the ground, we too have roots. Though they may not be as large, they grow and further deepen into the foundation of who we are. As I drifted deeper, I was able to identify my own self: I discovered my passions, strengths, and those undeniable weaknesses.

Exit: business major. Enter: public relations. I finally realized the business track I was on was trying to provide me with skills for the types of jobs I hated. I was passionate about writing and speaking, and other components of a communications major. I applied for Illinois State's College of Communications. As a junior, I knew it was going to be tough to get in. To say I was grateful when I got my acceptance letter would be the understatement of the year. I had completely failed as a business major. But in the college of PR and Communications, I excelled.

By nature, I am competitive. Ask anyone who plays Monopoly with me. And like most people, I hate losing and I hate failing, whether it is a game, project, task, or class. Nothing is more defeating than having to admit you are unable to do something. Looking back at the business school situation, I did everything in my power to succeed. I proved the phrase, "You can do whatever you put your mind to" to be sadly inaccurate. It is not easy to admit defeat, chalk up your efforts as failures, and move forward to a different course of action. However, that was my only option. It felt terrible, but I learned that while failure was inevitable, there was always an alternative option, even if it felt like a slightly less desirable one.

While failure most often times is the end of one path, it is the beginning of a new one. There is more than one road to get to your destination. I know when I am driving home from work, I have seven if not eight ways I could choose to get home. Each route has different components, aspects, variables, yet they all lead me to the same place. While your career is a winding road, there are multiple paths and sometimes you find yourself on a new one (much like when I did when I joined Orvin's new team at United Way in Chapter 3). And how amazing that gift can actually be. While I can fully admit that failing felt miserable, it opened my eyes to a completely new trajectory—one that continued to lead me down a whole new path. And for that, I am thankful.

Failing is never fun, but it is imperative to success. Failing creates new beginnings and new opportunities, which may bring additional failures but ultimately provides lessons.

Moving to Charlotte to open the company's office provided numerous challenges. In the beginning, the successes were minimal. Every day I would fail in setting a meeting. I would fail in selling our company's mission. I would fail in providing a solution to a prospect customer. However, each interaction and encounter would teach me how better to reach out, how better to respond, and how better to connect. Despite hundreds of mini failures, the overall initiative was a success.

Logically speaking, how do multiple failures still add up to success? Is the true equation for success "Challenges + Determination + Failure (+ Failure + Failure + Failure) – Giving Up"? Success means reaching one's goal or objective. In many cases, there are multiple routes to the destination of success and different pit stops along the way. And failing on one road needs to be the realization that a different course is available.

Look at your failures and see them solely as setbacks. Allow yourself to fail, then continue on. Everyone knows the comeback is always greater than any setback.

Failing is one of the least fun topics to discuss. Yet reflecting back on my failures, I have seen true growth in the form of skill development and in knowledge gained. I have not yet had an epic, defining moment of failure as Drew experienced in *Elizabethtown*. Maybe I never will. However, if I do, I hope to accept the experience with grace and to remain optimistically positive in my pursuit of success.

So, fail. Then wallow (briefly) in self-pity and enjoy a gallon of (insert guilty pleasure here ... donuts, cheese, ice cream, wine ...). And then ....

And then get up with grace and keep going. Don't allow your journey to end in an ellipsis ....

CHAPTER 12

Luck

My apartment in St. Louis did not have a thirteenth floor. John Mayer's *Room for Squares* album skipped track thirteen. And I have omitted a thirteenth chapter.

While I believe luck is mostly for the unprepared and desperate, I also believe it's for the hopeful. And it never hurts to have a little luck on your side. So, here's hoping for a little luck with this book that it may someday be a success, and to you and your future endeavors, that luck may be in your corner as well.

CHAPTER 14

Strategic Approach

You are assigned a new project. The first thing you do, whether you realize it or not, is create your approach. The approach is the way you progress, your methodology. Even if you do not consciously create an approach, your specific strategy moves you forward. Because having an approach is inevitable, make it a good one.

When faced with the decision of opening up a new office for a small IT company, I sat down with my CEO and my president. Together, we compiled a list of eight places that would be strong markets in which to work. Once the cities were decided upon, I was handed over the reins for the ultimate decision.

I was overwhelmed. I had to choose among eight very different yet equally appealing cities. While I was excited about a new adventure and challenge, I was unable to see past the decision of which city to pick. I fixated on each option, realizing any metropolitan area I chose would have a snowball effect on the rest of my life. And with each area having completely different characteristics, I felt like I was not only picking my new home, but also my entire destiny. And, how do you do that?

While trying to feel less overwhelmed (which felt nearly impossible), I created a strategic approach to analyze each city with factors that would benefit me personally and professionally. I left no topic untouched. I researched the number of Fortune 500 companies (for obvious reasons); number of competitors (sizing up my opponents); the ease of corporate relocation (expansion is always positive); the nearness of the airport (ease of corporate flying promotes executive presence); the organizations and boards in the area (self-explanatory); population of Millennials (a girl needs friends); the miles to drive home (because, family!); the ability to fly home (because, driving); favorite local activities people participated in (I like to have fun); the weather and climate (let's be serious, I hate the cold); and other similar factors. I put everything into a spreadsheet. I compared each area. Then, I traveled to my top four contenders.

Because the decision was one that felt like it would shape the entirety of my future, I took it extremely seriously. While my approach may have been slightly unconventional, it was what I needed to make a well-rounded decision. I know myself well enough that I know I need to be happy personally *and* professionally to succeed. And while there may be hardships on either side or times when one area might take precedence over the other, I need that work/life balance. This need to succeed became extremely transparent in my approach.

Creating an approach is an artful science. And it is entirely unique to different industries, geographical areas, and individuals. I've learned to distinguish which aspects prove to be successful in my approach and which are detrimental to the outcome.

> "BY ADAPTING YOUR APPROACH,
> YOU STRENGTHEN YOUR ABILITY
> TO MEET YOUR GOALS."

My approach proved to be successful, and I even surprised myself in my choice. In the end, I chose Charlotte, North Carolina as my destination and made my move.

When I moved to Charlotte, I had only been there two times previously—and that was counting the time I went there solely to sign my apartment lease. Why Charlotte? From all those factors I listed above, Charlotte had risen to the top. This city had room for national expansion and for companies to relocate, but had a strong base of companies already. It was listed as a top contender in national lists as a city for young professionals to move to, but it was also an American Airlines hub for easy travels back home. Weather promised to be warmer than the Midwest and it was close to the mountains but also, (more excitingly), the beach. Charlotte had a great vibe; it was welcoming, but it also had a lot to do. I saw so much potential in this city; it was still growing and evolving, and I felt I could help in this process. And to me, that was most exciting.

I felt relieved once I made my decision, however, I knew this was only the first step in a longer journey. I now had to create an approach to success. Success was such a broad word in this case, because it was truly all-encompassing. It included so many aspects such as: opening up our new office; obtaining clients; creating a network from scratch; and gaining credibility all while simultaneously building a social life, including making friends and finding hobbies.

Many people might have promoted a variety of ways to tackle what I had to do, but I designed a methodology that worked well for me. I created a three-prong approach to achieve my objectives. My three main focuses would be:

1. JOINING LOCAL BOARDS AND INITIATIVES;
2. ASKING FOR REFERRALS FROM CURRENT FRIENDS, COLLEAGUES, OR CLIENTS;
3. COLD OUTREACHES IN THE FORM OF LETTERS, CALLS, AND EMAILS.

Through these three interactions, I would utilize current relationships in which our reputation was already established and leverage the rule of numbers in cold-call outreaches. (Rule of numbers being that basically, the more calls made, the higher the success based off the shear fact that the odds were greater. But then again, I had failed calculus, remember?)

Overall, my strategy was successful. It neither stopped me from evaluating my efforts in terms of results, nor did it deter me from pursuing other ideas. One of the best things about having a conscientious approach is that as more knowledge and insight is obtained, the approach can evolve.

The ability to evolve a strategy is often overlooked. Along your way on the path to success, you may discover new perspectives and identify previously unknown factors that influence your thoughts and actions. By adapting your approach, you strengthen your ability to meet your goals.

Besides having no specific approach, the other detrimental situation in which you can find yourself is to have an approach written in stone, inflexible and unchanging. One of the most well-known stories that I believe proves how detrimental a static approach can be is that of Blockbuster.

I am sure we all know Blockbuster, the million-dollar conglomerate that owned the entire video-rental industry without much competition, and was untouchable with what was at first their highly-profitable approach. When at the time the lesser-known company, Netflix, reached out regarding a potential partnership, Blockbuster rejected them, feeling confident in their track record of success. While Netflix paved its way in an unlikely world, continuing to strive and adapting to consumers and new technology, Blockbuster refused to innovate and veer away from their approach.

Blockbuster is the epitome of stubbornness toward evolving one's approach. Obviously, this example is one of magnitude outcome. However, it shows the need and importance of creating and maintaining a strong approach.

Why is an approach so important? View your strategy as your roadmap to success. It is your guide to your endpoint. If you asked someone for directions and they gave you all the correct routes, turns, and detours, but provided them out of order, would you still reach your destination? Probably not. What if you asked someone for directions and this person told you all the correct information, but forgot to mention that a bridge along the way had collapsed, not offering any alternative route? Would you still reach your destination? Probably not. A strategic approach should not only be one that guides you to your desired goal, but is able to be flexible and evolve. Do not allow your approach to be rigid and uncompromising.

One strategic approach on which I have had a large focus is reaching out to individuals who I do not know in hopes of moving them through that fun little sales pipeline from prospect to client, AKA "cold calling, email edition." As such, I have turned quite frequently to a technique in reaching out to individuals in email form. In this regard, I write and receive a lot of emails all with one endgame in mind—setting a meeting to further discuss a product or service. Therefore, I am quite intrigued by the different methodologies and verbiage people use when they are going through this process.

Out of all the emails I receive from vendors, more than half have this starting line: "I know you are busy, but … " as in, I know you are busy, but I would love to tell you about my company/take you to lunch/invite you to explore our website, and so on. I have become captivated by the popularity of this opening statement and the outcomes it creates. As I speak with colleagues and friends about this approach, the response is consistently unanimous that this is not a very appealing line, and it does not encourage a reply.

I started to dissect the psychology behind this statement in terms of other settings. If you were to go on a blind date, would you introduce yourself like, "I know I have dandruff, but my eyes are beautiful"? Or would you buy something if you walked into a sporting goods store and the sales manager told you, "I know you are probably more of a football player, but I think you should buy these new irons"? Or when buying a new house, would you be sold if the relator stated, "I know the house has mold, but those crown moldings are to die for"?

100% times over and over again: NO. Just. No.

Why would you show someone an exit before even getting in the door? I started to refine my approaches with an undertone of confidence and exclusivity. Appeal to your prospect's interests, build them up, build yourself up. And a rule of thumb: if I objectively wouldn't take a meeting with myself after reading my email, I'm not going to send that email.

Another approach that has worked quite well for me is a strong subject line. I send emails to individuals with whom I hope to meet, using the subject line, "Coffee Tomorrow." I have had a great success rate with this subject line. It is eye-catching. It prompts people to wonder: Is she asking to meet for coffee tomorrow? Am I going to drink coffee tomorrow? Do we already have a meeting planned for coffee tomorrow? No one wants to miss a meeting. Once I capture my audience with this subject line, I need to continue to appeal to them in my message. This part is where I am constantly evolving and evaluating what I'm doing.

I don't know if anyone has truly cracked the code to a consistently successful email. Maybe there is no such formula, but I'm going to keep looking for it.

One strategy I have perfected with regards to prospecting is small talk. In this book, I mention large networking emails as well as one-on-one meetings. Small talk is consistently present in both scenarios. While some people make it easy to start conversations, others make it near impossible. Struggling to get a discussion going with your person of interest? Change your strategy.

Instead of just asking questions, encourage your person of interest to tell a story. Replace "How are you?" with "Tell me about your day." Exchange "Are you having a nice week?" with "What are you looking forward to this week?" It is mind-blowing how much more people will open up when prompted with the right question. And through asking thought-provoking, engaging questions, I was able to not only create a conversation, but to learn more about the individual.

There is no "one size fits all" strategy. The most important part of whatever you do is to find a way, not an excuse. It is easy to sit back and declare a situation an unresolvable issue. But no situation is. Create your move and take it. By defining your goal, your strategy will begin to reveal itself. Know your endgame and focus in on it with the precision of a laser. As you continue on your journey of success, remember to allow your strategy to evolve and your methodology to adapt. Otherwise your story, (hopefully unlike mine), could become one just for the books. And, as with Blockbuster, we all know how that story goes.

CHAPTER 15

Empower Yourself

"What doesn't kill you makes you stronger."

Inhale. Exhale. Are you empowered? No? Me neither.

In the workplace, our talk about empowerment may be limited to some motivational poster or inspirational quote slapped onto the wall in the break room. And yet empowerment and success go hand in hand. I've reflected quite a bit on the notion of empowerment, and I find it to be intriguing. Empowering people is more than simply saying the right string of words or looking at a positive picture. It is the science of motivating a person to *feel compelled* to do something. (Emphasis on to *feel*.) I've learned not only do different people empower me at different times, but different seasons of life call for different purposes of passion. I have never been a person to to struggle with self-confidence. (I more so suffer from the opposite, and I have to ask, is anyone else with me there? Let's expand.)

I have been and continue to be a confident individual. Even when I am wrong (which I clearly never am, insert face palm emoji), it takes me a while to admit it because I am too busy convincing you (and myself) that I am still right. Where does that wonderfully-positive, confident demeanor take its nasty little turn into egocentric, cocky narcissism? Honestly, I don't know. And if I hate anything as much as being wrong, it is not knowing.

Going back to the discussion on authenticity and self-awareness, I believe there is a fine line between negative and positive connotations of confidence. And sometimes, it is simply less about how you portray the term and more about how others observe it. So, be confident. Lean in, stand up for opinions. But also learn to balance and recalibrate when you're swaying too far to one side.

"TALK ABOUT YOUR FAILURES.
TALK ABOUT YOUR CHALLENGES.
STOP WITH THE FLUFFY RAINBOW AND
SPARKLES AND TELL ME THAT *REAL* REAL."

⌒⌒

Coupling hand in hand with confidence, I have never needed reassurance from other people to validate my work efforts. Mostly, I know when my work is high-quality—meaning I also know when a project is not. I know some individuals need the "Good jobs!" and the "You're doing greats!" along the way. But I simply don't. I do not believe either way is right or wrong—I think it is personal preference. I've managed some individuals who simply hate these comments, while on the other hand, I've managed others who need them, thrive off of them, use them as motivational guides. However, despite my independent, self-assured demeanor, I still have my moments of weakness where I need inspiration to continue my journey. I am still in the process of developing how to verbalize these moments, (though sometimes they simply dissipate on a long, much-needed night run), but I am willing to invest in myself to learn.

What I have realized about reassurance is the importance of being real. Talk about your failures. Talk about your challenges. Stop with the fluffy rainbow and sparkles and tell me that *real* real.

⌒⌒

After being in Charlotte for five exciting months, I successfully brought on multiple new clients, made some fabulous friendships, and created amazing contacts. But the newness was wearing off and the fact I was alone in a new metropolitan area was sinking in. Meeting rejections from people refusing to become clients, something that had never before fazed me (it is all a part of sales, right?), were starting to defeat my mindset. I approached my boss, in hopes of a pep talk, but received questions about my lack of appointments. Salt in the wound. I was trying to get more. Any advice? Guidance? Help? My friends, both new and old, kept assuring me I was doing great, but they didn't really understand (or so I kept telling myself). My family was fabulous and and supported me. (Did they have a choice?) My lackluster outlook was increasing, and I was trying (wallowing, drowning, grasping) to find something or someone to reenergize me, inspire me, empower me. I was in a full-blown, reservation for one, just love me, pity party.

And then, I met Grant Cardone.

Well, I didn't actually *meet* him (yet), but I found his book, *The 10X Rule*. And it was just what I needed at just the right time. It called attention to the fact I was lacking in results not because of all I was doing, but because of some of the things I was *not* doing. It denied me the ability to use excuses as factors in failing. Instead it put the accountability on one person: me.

I read the book in a matter of days. Then I reread it. I created an approach consisting of action items. *The 10X Rule* became my working manual, guiding me through my challenges and struggles. In a business lull, I found empowerment from a place of education. The book enabled me to refocus my strategy. It showed me if I wanted success, I could make it happen. Did I already know some of the things Grant told me? Absolutely. But it was just what I needed to hear in the way I needed to hear it. Preach.

Empowerment comes in different waves at different times. I cannot be the only one who puts on my headphones and walks down the street with a random song blaring for only me to hear (strongly suggesting Lord Huron's "She Lit A Fire" or Florence + the Machine's "Shake It Out"). How can you not gain at least a small pep in your step with a personal soundtrack to instill confidence?

I was in Atlanta not too long ago for a second meeting with Ed, a leader at Coca-Cola. We spoke for an hour about the importance of networks (his is truly impressive) and the importance of creating a relationship with clients/prospects.

I left with an overload of thoughts and ideas swimming in my head. I tried to write down as many as I could remember and proceeded to decipher through them. As I began to drive four hours back to Charlotte, I was so lost in thought, I didn't realize until I was home that I had driven in complete silence.

This was the type of meeting that had not only left me inspired, but had also empowered me. I was energized to put our discussion into action. I was motivated to connect with other leaders and to cultivate new relationships. It was a meeting that had pushed *me* to push harder in pursuit of my quarterly (as well as career) goals.

I thought more about the definition of the word "empowered." And while I found the term to be inspirational, I also found it oddly passive. I had been empowered by a conversation with Ed. I had been empowered through reading Grant's book.

There is a reason why keynote speakers tend to err on the side of motivational—to make you feel empowered! But simply sitting in a large auditorium, nodding along to profound statements, cannot force you to put foot to pavement. It is you alone who needs to empower yourself to do what you need to do.

It is well-known that all too often, people (myself included) will pass their failures on to other people. I addressed this issue and the importance of taking ownership for your shortcomings in an earlier chapter. It is easy to sit back and say your sales weren't met because of the holiday season, or you were late to work because the stoplights were all red. Passing off failures is something with which people are familiar. However, why do we rarely address the lack of ownership for our own empowerment?

While I realize sometimes it takes a match to light the fuse, I also believe we keep burning on our own regard. No individual person, place, or thing directly told me to write this book. (But let me tell you, too many times I even tried to discourage myself from writing it!) However, I empowered myself to do it anyway. I did not have to move to Charlotte to open up the company's new office; I empowered myself to do it.

If I had stayed in St. Louis, working with the same company, continuing my same job, I am sure I would still be in a role, there or elsewhere, at which I'd be decent. However, I wanted to experience a new challenge and push myself to grow in other areas. While conversations with my bosses, family, colleagues, and friends were extremely insightful, there was one person who inspired and provoked the change. Me.

I get it—this is once again easier said than done. "Let me just empower myself to do these endless mundane tasks I sadly call my job ...." Am I right? No. If this was your reaction, this chapter is exactly what you need. Don't love your job, but not in a place to leave it? Find your purpose outside of your 9 a.m. to 5 p.m. existence. Volunteer for a nonprofit, sit on a board, participate in an activity you love. A lack of empowerment leads to a decrease in productivity, an absence of passion, and a fast track to failure.

⚬⚭⚬

Throughout the years, I have had numerous moments of self-doubt and self-pity, to which I learned the only real cure was feeling empowered. One of the most important aspects of empowerment is to take full accountability of your actions. Don't allow yourself to be the victim. When you victimize yourself, you no longer have power or influence. Your energy becomes visibly toxic. Instead, take full responsibility for the things you do, and it will lead you to do things you are proud of. Refusing to allow yourself to play the victim will instill a level of confidence that truly exudes empowerment.

Need some extra help? Another aspect and a truly golden realization was when I learned to get to know myself in regard to my motivators. Conversations with mentors and admired leaders; inspirational podcasts that provoked change, and more importantly action; and creating positive change, were all ways in which I empowered myself. Different things for different seasons, however, I have learned that by thinking back to or partaking in newly constructive and insightful situations or conversations, I feel empowered.

Sometimes I need to just get out of the four walls that feel like they are closing in on me and take a walk. I find serenity in reflecting on my objectives and the steps I am taking to achieve them.

In my office, I have a variety of accessories and décor. (It is all extremely trendy and cute, by the way. Thank you very much Kate Spade and Target! ... P.S. Yes, I have a gold stapler.) However, a few items serve a bigger purpose than to simply fill space on the shelf or wall. They actually fill the space where my self-doubt used to live.

I have a globe on my desk that is a constant and tangible reminder that the world is bigger than any problem I am experiencing. When I struggle with an obstacle that feels like it is drowning my spirits, I can look at the world and remember it is all about perspective. I feel empowered to know that as I work hard to succeed, others work hard to survive. While this may seem dramatic, it is the inspiration that I sometimes not only appreciate, but need to keep me going through my workday.

A picture frame also sits on my desk. In the frame is a scrap of tarnished paper that was cut out of a news article and has one statement that never ceases to inspire me. "If you see someone without a smile, give him yours."

This sentiment is meaningful to me in countless ways. The piece of paper came from the workshop previously owned by my hardworking, successful, and slightly ego-centric grandpa. This quote reiterates the importance of kindness and shows that a smile goes a long way. More importantly, it reminds me that hard work and willpower pay off. Unfortunately, I lost my grandpa when I was seven years old, yet the similarities in our personalities are undeniable. So, I thank him for my determination (while simultaneously cursing him for my stubbornness).

I also have a bookshelf filled with books to read or lend out or review; awards I have won; mementos from fellow meetings/events/programs; and about four pairs of heels in which to stand tall. Above the bookshelf is a bulletin board covered with thank you cards, ticket stubs, name tags, and notes. All of these items are little reminders that help carry me through days when I need a little empowerment.

One silly phrase I have perhaps awkwardly begun living is, "Your day, your way." Whether it is your birthday (because then it really is a your-day-your-way situation), a stressful Friday or, as mentioned earlier, a much-needed spa day, do *you*. Enable yourself to feel empowerment through whatever means you have.

Allow yourself to feel inspired by the conversations you have and the places you go. Regardless of the person, place, quote, or speck of dust that enables you to empower yourself, learn it, love it, and embrace it. Because at the end of it all, it truly is your day, your way.

CHAPTER 16

What Now, What Next

How many times have you watched an amazing TV season on Netflix and, after the finale, where you go through this whirlwind of events, with the riveting climax turning into a life-changing resolution, and as the credits float up the screen, you sit there astounded, look around the room, and ask no one in particular, "What next?"

This scenario is my life in a nutshell (minus the riveting climax or the life-changing resolution ... yet). I have thrown myself (notice the non-passive verbiage there ...) into the world of business and while after each compelling interaction, victorious moment, or successful meeting, I am left with the same question that brought me to write this book in the first place: "What next?"

As I continue to propel myself further into this crazy corporate affair, I have learned I am asking myself the entirely wrong question. Instead of "What next?" I should be focused on "What now?"

I am sure most people have heard the quote, "There is no better time than the present." Take this statement and incorporate it into your every-day life.

Too many times, after finishing a discussion, chapter, event, or whatever, I get overwhelmed with my thoughts, and I start compiling my research for next steps. Think about all those occasions when you've constructed a "to-do" list. How often have you assembled your list, only to spend the majority of your effort writing it instead of actually working to complete it? Several times, I have created my lists complete with fancy artwork and visuals. But do not allow yourself to get stuck in the "to-do/what next" planning phase. Looking at a situation from a "what next" perspective can feel overwhelming. Essentially, it is about planning the plan. But when you change your approach to "what now," it forces you to move on to the execution of your plan.

> "DO NOT ALLOW YOURSELF TO GET STUCK
> IN THE 'TO-DO/WHAT NEXT' PLANNING PHASE
> ... WHEN YOU CHANGE YOUR APPROACH
> TO 'WHAT NOW,' IT FORCES YOU TO MOVE ON
> TO THE EXECUTION OF YOUR PLAN."

When I first planned to open a new office for the IT company, the situation seemed like a dream come true. While inquiring about the different steps I would need to take and creating a list of tasks to complete, I realized it was the notion of execution that enabled me to make the move to North Carolina. Multiple times a week, my superiors and colleagues asked me if the move was really going to happen. The first two weeks of discussion had mostly just focused on conceptualizing and brainstorming. Which, honestly, could have easily continued as time has a way of turning weeks into months into maybe this isn't such a good idea. However, after those two weeks of planning, I made the adamant decision to move when I signed a lease that was move-in ready, from signature on the lease to key in hand in just fourteen days. That means it was one month, from idea to execution; from muttering the words "move" to driving that U-Haul trailer across four state lines. The realization I needed to do something now prompted me to change my to-do list from "what next" to "what now."

Moving from the "next" to the "now" is not as easy as signing a lease or flipping the page and starting your new journey. Therefore, I've found when I am stuck in between the two, standing in limbo, I ask myself, "Why?" Whether it is the fear of the unknown, the perplexity of the situation, the anxiety of failure, or the high workload, identifying and then understanding the obstacle helps to lessen its intensity.

So, you've read this book. It changed your mindset. What now? Now you implement the concepts you have learned. You apply your knowledge. You challenge yourself and grow in your learning. You fail. Then, you start again.

Allow yourself to live the big life for which you are destined. Give yourself permission to dream big and follow through. Flirt with the boundaries of your comfort zone and force yourself outside of them because that's where all the fun happens—that's where you grow, fail, learn.

There is no formula for success (although I did try to create one in Chapter 11). Nor is there a secret playbook to guide you on your journey (if you're upset or surprised, I tried to warn you in the beginning). What you do have, however, is the knowledge to point you forward. Would you make it out of a hidden forest alone with no tools? Maybe. Would it be easier with a compass pointing you north? Absolutely. Just obtaining the compass would do nothing, though. You need to learn how to read it, use it, and follow it. This is the same with success. When you equip yourself with the knowledge to succeed, you will have a much easier time navigating through the winding journey.

I find it encouraging that there are things I can do now to progress in my career. By putting in the extra five hours a week, sending an additional fifty emails, or attending one networking event that lasts too long, I am invoking my own evolution.

One week, I was booked in endless meetings around the clock. I had obligations every night, and I was beginning to drag. I had a networking event I knew was going to be crowded, long, and overwhelming. No one would have known if I had decided to skip the cocktail reception and opted instead for a long workout followed by a warm bubble bath. Very tempting, but the temptation was not strong enough. Growing up, watching my mom get up at the crack of dawn to do laundry and stay up until midnight to help type papers, inspired me to continue to put in that extra effort.

Much to my despair, I ended up putting on my little black dress and my stilettos and was off to the party. The event ended up being everything I needed and more. In a time when I was running around mindlessly, engaging in countless conversations, I walked into a room where I could just be still. The week flew by me, and I was too busy to notice that while my discussions had been productive, they had lacked meaning and personality.

Throughout the evening, I was able to reconnect with more than eight of my key prospects, three of whom I had met with previously in the week. I learned about alma maters, children's ages, a shared love of long-distance running, hometowns that were hours away in proximity, local favorites, and more. I was able to solidify discussions, but more importantly, I fostered growing relationships in a lighthearted environment.

I left that night with a little pep in my step. Yes, it would have been easy to take the night off and relax. However, despite my whirlwind of a week, I realized the need to put in additional effort.

There are ebbs and flows in all aspects of life, business, and activities. When making the decision to put in the extra effort or take a day off, make the right choice for the situation. Sometimes, rest and relaxation are needed to rejuvenate and reenergize. Be educated on your process and your progress so that when you are faced with making these choices, you can do so with conscientious thought and knowledge.

Reflecting on the cocktail reception, I knew I was still new to the area and needed to continue to put forth extra effort to succeed. That additional effort was just one of the little things I did "in the now" that enabled me to continue onward toward my goal of success.

᠊᠊᠊

When I am home in the Quad Cities for the holidays, I enjoy spending time with my family. Much to my brother Charlie's dislike, taking pictures is a huge part of the festivities. And by pictures I don't mean one or two—I mean more along the lines of 870, give or take. But in today's fabulous world with all the technology at our fingertips and social media at every turn of the corner, what good is a picture if you don't post it? Because philosophically speaking ... if a picture wasn't posted on Instagram, did it really happen? (No, but seriously. Did it?)

So, in my family, who all live dispersed across four separate cities, getting together and taking pictures ranks up high on our list of activities (right below games, eating, and laughing but right above drinking gentlemen drinks). Every time someone (usually my sister or I) would take out a camera phone to take/upload a picture, my brother-in-law, Jeff, would without fail shout, "Live in the now!"

The man's got a point. "Live in the now" is a phrase that needs to be reiterated in all areas of life, including in business. When posting pictures instead of living them, or when planning a book tour before publishing a book, you are simply focusing on the future that is figuratively built; it is not a guarantee.

Speaking of books, here is a funny story: I wrote this one three years before I decided to accept the offer I was given to get it published. There was intent, followed by interest, but then life hit. I was offered my dream job, to lead a sports foundation and be the head of CSR (Corporate Social Responsibility), for a professional sports team. This role combined everything I had learned thus far along with presenting new challenges and opportunities I had striven to one day have. The job has provided—and continues to provide—so much, but there is still so much more.

So, I continue on. Stuffing my insecurities deep inside one pocket and my fears in the other, I keep my head held high and push on. Our paths are paved through the choices we make and the opportunities we pursue. We are each building our own story, one brick at a time. Make it one worth telling. Better yet—make it one worth reading.

As you venture on your own journey, keep yourself in the present. Focus on what you can do now. Don't think about next week, month, year. While in this "messy middle" phase of your career journey, concentrate on where your attention is needed now, in this precise moment. And when you triumphantly complete one goal, simply cross it off your list, smile as you think about what is next, and then ask yourself, "What now?"

CHAPTER 17

To Be Continued ...

My story, while no longer at the beginning, is far from over. I have introduced myself to you, but I look forward to continuing this pleasant courtship.

Whether I succeed in my goals or you succeed in yours, our stories are now intertwined. I look forward to continuing my story as you continue yours.

With dedication and a strong work ethic, your goals are attainable. And while your goals might currently be (however so slightly) out of your grasp, be proud that you are striving and succeeding while in

mid-reach.